The Jesse James Scrapbook

A Novel By

George Jansen

HILLIARD Harris
PUBLISHERS

Published by

HILLIARD  HARRIS
PUBLISHERS

P.O. Box 3358
Frederick, Maryland 21705-3358

The Jesse James Scrapbook Copyright © 2003 by George Jansen

First Edition

ISBN 1-59133-031-9

Designed by HILLIARD HARRIS

Cover Illustration © S.A. Reilly
Cover design by S. A. Reilly

Manufactured/Printed in the United States of America
2003

Dedication

"for the dear departed"

Acknowledgements

I would like to thank Lora Fountain, Bryan Costales, Dave Singleton, and Sue Clark for their work as critics and editors. Lora helped me discover the book I really wanted to write. Bryan made it "faster and shorter." Dave refused to let me take the easy way out. Sue understood what the book really was and got me over the hump.

Thanks also to Kathy Ronay Birdsong, Jeanne McKay, Helen Scharmer, Rick Shubb, Jane Strong, Cathy Trinidad, and Mitty Varadan for their help and encouragement. And last, but hardly least, a special thanks to Marcia Savin, whose most excellent teachings caused me to embark on the perilous quest that brought me here.

PROLOGUE

Summer 1906

Tom Gardner, age twelve, hoisted himself to the top of Old Man Ginty's fence and eyeballed his chances. Neither Ginty, his dogs, nor his ferocious rooster were in evidence. All that stood between Tom and triumph, were the beehives, the goldfish pond, and a picket fence so low it filled him with contempt.

"Afternoon, Tom."

From out of nowhere Old Man Ginty appeared, a hatchet in his hand.

Tom leaped into the yard, sucked down a healthy dose of air, and churned his legs like the great drivers of a steam locomotive. He accelerated past the beehives, leaped the fish pond, and scrambled over the picket fence. He flew across the trolley tracks and almost collided with the Long Island City electric. He took the stairs of his house by threes, threw open the front door, and launched himself into a belly-slide down the polished, hardwood floor.

"Safe," he cried.

But just as he crashed into the umbrella stand, the joyous, summer air was rent by a voice as furious and frightful as a rolling clap of thunder.

"Thompson Grant Gardner!"

In a flash, Tom took it all in. His mother's arms were folded across her chest. Her features were contorted in a hideous sneer. Pressed to her bosom was an item that had heretofore been buried in his bureau under a pile of brownish baseballs and old, smelly socks—The Jesse James Scrapbook.

"What's the meaning of this, Tom?" his mother said, her hand upon the book.

"I just pitched a shutout," he replied, in a desperate bid for time. "Had my in-shoot, had my out-shoot, had my false-rise, and those Maspeth boys didn't have a prayer."

"There's no dodging it, Tom."

Trapped, he hung his head. "Your things are still in there, Ma. I just pasted over 'em."

"You pasted your Jesse James over my Tour of the Continent?"

Tom got to his feet.

"It was a long time ago," he lied. "We were just kids playing games. We were detectives, you see, even had our own detective agency. We swore a blood oath to capture Robert Ford, the coward who assassinated Jesse James, and we had to have evidence so we could get a warrant..."

"Come to the point, Tom."

"I am. I am."

Though the role of traitor and informer fit the infamous Ford better than he, was it not written that the strong would survive and the weak would perish?

"It was Jumbo that did it. Jumbo went to the library, and..."

"Don't try to blame it on poor Jumbo."

"I ain't, Ma. I ain't."

Jumbo was a fat, dyspeptic boy, and, as such, Tom realized, he was the recipient of unwarranted sympathy from little old ladies and mothers alike.

"It was George that was at the bottom of it," Tom declared, altering course just enough to launch an all out attack on his older brother.

"George made himself a colonel. I only made myself a captain even though the Wide Awakes was all my idea. Poor Jumbo went to the library because George said to. He cut things out of newspapers and books because George said to."

"You know..." His mother paged through the book. "Some of the parts you wrote yourself are really quite good."

"Thanks, Ma. I thought so, too."

"'After the Civil War,'" she read, "'Jesse James surrendered his arms and attempted to return to the pursuits of peace. But his old enemies and the Yankee militia still had it in for him. They hounded Jesse and persecuted him till all he had left was the outlaw life. So he took to the woods with his merry men, and there they lived a carefree existence—hunting, fishing, and engaging in target practice...'"

She looked at him. "Why don't you write this well on your compositions?"

"I do, but the teachers are prejudiced against me. Mr. Sheckard's a Dutchman, you know."

"The word is German. Not Dutchman."

"Mr. Sheckard's a German, and German's are all prejudiced against Americans."

"Why, that's nonsense, Tom. Who ever told you that?"

"Pa did."

His mother fell into a confused silence, and Tom, knowing he had struck a telling blow, sent a regiment of cavalry through the breach in her lines.

"'All Germans are good for,'" quoth Tom, "'is drinking beer and preaching anarchy. If it weren't for the Germans...'"

"That's not true, Tom, and you know it. Sometimes your father gets angry when he reads the papers and says things he doesn't mean."

"Jesse James never touched off any anarchist bomb. Jesse James robbed from the rich and gave to the poor. He fought on the side of justice and right."

"Jesse James," his mother said, "was a killer and thief. We've talked before about that trash you boys read."

"I've stopped readin' it, too, Ma, and I'm a better boy for it, I'll say."

3

His mother sighed a deep, tormented sigh. "You know you'll have to be punished for this, and I'll have to let Jumbo's mother know too."

"But it wasn't Jumbo Brown, Ma," Tom said, with noble purpose. "It was some other fellow named Jumbo. He never told us his last name. All we ever knew him by was Jumbo."

"You boys," his mother continued, "have stolen books and newspapers from the library."

"We took 'em back."

"After you'd cut pages out."

"Yes, ma'm."

"You took my scrapbook without permission, young man, and when your father gets home, there will be hell to pay."

She laid The Jesse James Scrapbook on the hall table, righted the fallen umbrella stand and pointed a trembling forefinger at the stairs.

"To your room."

Tom slunk toward the stairs, and, as he did, the staircase seemed to take on the aspect of a gallows. When he reached the first step, he turned and faced the woman who had appointed herself judge and jury.

"Ma? What are you planning to do with the book? I know I did wrong, but I worked real hard on it. I never did finish it, but someday I'm going to, even if it takes a hundred years. I'm going to go out west and interview farmers and outlaws and trainmen and wild Indians, everyone who ever knew or saw or was robbed by Jesse. You wouldn't burn a fellow's life's work, would you?"

"You should have thought of that before you borrowed my scrapbook. And if you've started contemplating your life's work, young man, I suggest you begin by ruling out both Jesse James and baseball."

He looked towards the top of the stairs and imagined his father standing there—an executioner's mask covered his face, a razor strop was in his hands. A cold drizzle was falling.

Jesse James, Tom knew, wouldn't have quailed. Jesse James would have met his fate with a stout heart and an enigmatic smile.

4

Young Tom Gardner threw back his shoulders and climbed.

WAR

1

Spring 1850
Billy Drury, Farmer
Clay County, Missouri

Up in Liberty, just north of my place, the citizens employed a
bugler who blew taps at sunset to let the slaves know it was
time to get off the street. Ever since I could remember, that
bugler had spouted off—taps at sunset, reveille at sunrise—and
an awful thing it was. I heard that bugle, but turned a deaf
ear—sold my corn, sold my hemp, took the money and was
glad of it.

Yes, I knew Jesse's pa.

The Reverend Robert James, that would be. He lived about
fifteen miles from here, up near Kearney. Had a decent sized
place. Grew corn and hemp like most of us. Kept a half-dozen
slaves, but I can't tell you how he reconciled such a practice
with Christian charity. He did ride circuit around here, founded
a church or two and was forever holding revivals.

My little farm was down by the river—by the crossroads,
near the ferry—so it was natural enough for him to stop by
every now and again.

"Ain't seen you up to New Hope Baptist since your wife
died, Mr. Drury."

"No, guess you ain't."

Big fellow, he was. Tall like Frank. Handsome like Jesse. Every time I turned around back then, seemed like, there was the Reverend James, sitting atop his black mare, looking down his nose at me.

"How's Tom Jeff comin' along?" he'd ask. I owned a thoroughbred horse named Thomas Jefferson, in those days.

"Tom Jeff's comin' along fine," I'd say. "How's the wife and children?"

"My wife is always well, and Frank is a quick learner. Care to sell him, Mr. Drury? Tom Jeff, I mean."

Most fearsome thing about the Reverend were his eyes—like iron, they were—and a somber sight, he could be—in his black suit, on his black horse—with those eyes fixed dead on you.

"No 'hoppers this year, praise God," he'd say.

"Yes sir, no 'hoppers," I'd reply. "Praise God," I might add, just to cover my tracks.

One fine day in the spring of eighteen and fifty, I was out cultivating my little vegetable garden—beans, carrots, cabbage—you know. The sparrows were a-twitterin' and the bees were a-buzzin'. It was one of those glorious days of days when you knew old man winter was done for at last and you just felt like singing out loud.

Then, somehow, the Reverend James, on that big black mare of his, managed to sneak up behind me.

"Afternoon, Mr. Drury."

My heart jumped about a foot. It was all very strange. The dogs hadn't even barked.

"How's Tom Jeff doin'?" he asked.

"Tom Jeff's doin' fine," I said, my heart pounding a tattoo.

"Still ain't seen you up to New Hope Baptist."

"No, you still ain't."

He shifted around in his saddle and made himself comfortable.

"I been considerin' going out to California," he said, staring at me all hard-eyed. "Save a few souls, maybe. Pan a little gold, maybe. What do you think? The adventure of a lifetime, I'd say."

"Ain't a bad idea," I told him. Thousands were doing it. Argonauts they called themselves and as green as green could be, they were.

"Shouldn't be all that difficult," the Reverend said. "I've purchased a guide book."

"Capt'n Fremont's?"

"Precisely," he said. "And I have prayed over it."

Some folks say the real reason the Reverend James headed west was because his wife was cheating on him, but I never believed that. Nor do I believe that little Jess clung to his legs and pleaded for him to stay, like other folks say. Jess would have been but two or three years old at the time. It could have happened that way, I suppose, but I don't know for sure. I didn't pay much mind to those boys back then, to tell the truth.

"I'll be back in a year or two," the Reverend told me. "My pockets will be bursting and the future assured."

He never did come back. Dysentery, it could have been. Cholera, maybe. Jess went looking for his grave after he growed up, but I don't think he ever found it. Can't say for sure. You know how men are. Jess never talked much about the experience and I never asked.

His ma remarried a few years after the Reverend died. But I can't tell you much about that fellow, either. I first met him over in Keatsville, when I was selling my hemp to Sidney Marion Keats. Sid had a ropewalk on his plantation up there, you see. He was the one who introduced us.

"Billy Drury, say hello to Dr. Reuben Samuel."

"Mr. Drury," Dr. Samuel said, smiling.

He seemed the exact opposite of the Reverend—not overbearing in the least, but calm, I'd say. Pleasant, even.

"Glad to meet you, doctor," I said, as we shook hands. He had a decent enough grip, as I recall.

"My pleasure," he said. "Absolutely."

He never practiced medicine after he married, don't know why—preferred farming, I suppose.

"Care to have a look around, gentlemen?" Sid Keats asked. Red haired and dapper was how Sid looked—a genuine, dyed in the wool, Southern cavalier. During the war, he became a great general and, afterwards, an ardent supporter of Frank and Jesse James, but he was still just Sid Keats, in those days.

"We've made some big improvements since your last visit, Billy. You might want to see them."

I told him no thank you.

I'd toured his ropewalk once, you see, and once was enough. It stood about a mile off from the plantation house—out of sight, like a snake in the meadow. A thousand feet long, it was, because the weaving of the rope had to be done in a straight line. The hemp was spun into yarn, and the yarn was twisted into long strands. Then the slaves would tie these strands to their waists, and walk back and forth all day long, three hundred groaning spiders, weaving the hemp—my hemp—into rope.

"Dr. Samuel?" Sid Keats said. "Care to have a look around?"

"Yes. Certainly. Never having seen it before, and since we're going to be doing business."

"You're sure, Billy?"

I shook my head, no. "I'll just set on the porch and enjoy the peace, if you don't mind."

The back porch of Sid's plantation house, the verandah, he called it, overlooked the flower gardens and the lawn. It was lovely sitting there, watching the black women weed and the black men mow. I made myself comfortable and a boy brought me hot tea and corn battercakes from the cookhouse.

Skinny, he was, and barefoot, wearing nothing but a man-sized shirt that hung down to his knees. I asked him how old he was, but he just smiled and backed away.

"Ten?" I said. "Eleven?"

When he grinned I saw how bad his teeth were—worse than mine, even.

"The South has been a colony of the North too long," Sid Keats said later on, as we sipped our tea on his doomed veranda.

Dr. Samuel seconded the motion. "It's time we stood up for our rights. What do you say, Mr. Drury? We can't back down, now. Can we?"

"Don't know much about politics," I said.

Sid Keats shook his head. "This isn't about politics, Billy. It's about freedom. Missouri cannot be free unless Kansas is slave. You can understand that, can't you?"

Kansas was getting ready to come into the Union about that time, as I recall. Slave state, free state, it didn't matter much to me.

"But the Puritans are trying to impose their will on us, Billy. They're coming down from Massachusetts to stuff the ballot boxes. You don't like Puritans, do you?"

"Don't know any Puritans."

Dr. Samuel shook his head. "You wouldn't like them if you did."

Later on, Sid passed by my place on his way to the ferry. Had a few friends with him—two or three hundred would be my guess—mounted, angry and armed to the teeth.

Sid called out to me from atop the fine-blooded charger he rode. "You going with us, Billy?"

"Well, what kind of picnic is this?" I said, standing safe inside my garden. "And where are you going anyway?"

"We're going to Kansas to vote," Sid Keats said.

"Vote? Why you're Missourians. How can you vote in Kansas? And what are you carrying all those guns for?"

Sid Keats laughed. "Your second question answers your first. We're paying a dollar a day plus whiskey. Are you with us, sir? Or are you against us?"

I heard wild-eyed John Brown preach in Lawrence, Kansas, once. A regular fortified town, Lawrence was in those days—it got burned out in fifty-five, as I recall, then again by Quantrill in sixty-three. Frank was in on that raid. Cole Younger was, too. Some folks say Jesse was there, others say he wasn't. He was only fifteen or so, at the time. But I can't tell you the truth of that, either—damn lot of good, I am. It just ain't the kind of question a wise man asks of Jesse James, you see.

Don't matter, one way or the other, though. Jess murdered and pillaged with the best of them, once he was given the chance. And as for John Brown, well, he was just about as crazy as any Southern cavalier you might care to mention.

"Without the shedding of blood," cried he, "there is no remission from sin. One Sharp's rifle will have more effect on the slavers than a thousand Bibles."

That was when the shooting started—the guerrilla war on the Kansas-Missouri border. Folks killed each other, ran off each others stock and burned each others farms. Once it got started there was no stopping it.

"Are you with us, sir? Or are you against us?"

I was born the same year Dan'l Boone died, by the way. First president I have much recollection of was Andy Jackson. Yes sir, Andy was president, and the common man was king when I was a boy.

Frank and Jesse, they weren't so lucky.

2
Autumn 1856
Ophelia Helms, Schoolteacher
Clay County, Missouri

At the end of the school year in 1856 I was let go from my teaching position in Gallatin, Missouri. But that did not surprise me one bit for teaching, in those days, was something of a nomadic profession. School districts, for reasons I never agreed with, preferred bringing in new teachers every few years to keeping the old ones. I was twenty-four years old and, having begun teaching when I was sixteen, I had already held five different positions.

I applied for employment in Clay County, Missouri. A horrible guerrilla war was raging nearby on the Kansas border, but I don't suppose anyone ever considers that the sweep of history will have the slightest effect on them. I was trying to get work to keep body and soul together and in that there was difficulty enough.

As is well known, the respectable occupations for women in those days were teaching school or teaching music, but even so, male teachers were preferred. The big boys, it was feared, would run wild with nothing but a woman—and especially a diminutive one—between them and the devil. Thus, both my gender and small size counted against me as did the fact that I had reached such an advanced age and had yet to marry.

So I lied to the school board.

I told them I was engaged and that my intended was surveying a railroad route to California. He was to return in two years, I said, and then we would be married. This tale quelled their fears and impressed them, too, as railroading was quite the thing in those days, and I was given the job.

The schoolhouse where I was to both teach and live was a lovely, white, clapboard building standing in a secluded grove near Kearney. It was a one-room school of the type our poets and politicians are fond of romanticizing about. I, however, knew what to expect. I brought with me the four McGuffy's Readers I owned, a roll of maps, a dictionary, my precious globe of the world, and an old alarm clock.

Let the poets dwell on the merits of the one-room school, I shall not. That fall I had seventy students and not a single, proper desk. The students sat on benches so high that the younger children's legs could not touch the floor and, so, dangled in space, all day. The school's library consisted of a Bible and a Farmer's Almanac, and many of the children did not have the money to buy slates and writing tablets.

We did not have grades in those days, the students, instead, were placed according to the reader they were using. My seventy scholars were spread out over eight readers, first through eighth. One lone teacher—man or woman—doubling as janitor, nurse, and handyman, besides could not cope with such circumstances, and it was necessary, then, for the older students to help the younger ones.

Frank James was one of the helpers, Jesse one of the helped.

I do not mean to imply that Jesse James was a poor student or dull in any way. He was nine or so, and in the fourth reader just as he should have been. Frank was about twelve or thirteen and very advanced. He did, upon occasion, become overwrought when his performance was less than perfect but, by and large, he was my prize pupil.

I do not believe I ever met their stepfather. If I did he made no lasting impression on me, but I remember the boy's mother, Mrs. Samuel—a mule of a woman, as all we western women had to be. Still, she was more educated than most men, and her library was much more extensive than any of the other parent's. She had strong political views, and, though we disagreed on Abolition, it gladdened my heart to meet a woman who did not shrink from such discussions.

"We paid good money for our darkies," she once told me. "If the Yankees want to free 'em so bad, they can buy 'em from us. And how would we grow our hemp and corn? Read Ephesians VI, 5, if you want to know the word of God."

She did seem to dote a bit on Frank—or Mr. Frank, as she called him—and, in truth, I remember him much better than I do Jesse. Jesse I remember as being very fond of horses but not much different from the other boys. He was a regular boy I should say. In the years since he became famous, I've read tales that he, as a child, tortured small animals and did hideous things to his classmates. But those stories are untrue, of course, being nothing more than the imaginings of the authors of cheap, paperback books.

If anything, the childhoods of Frank and Jesse, and of all the children who attended that lonely school near Kearney, were much more frightening than anything a dime novelist could ever invent. I think I would have been better able to cope with a lone boy killing a cat, let us say, than with what actually transpired.

I recall standing at a window during first recess one spring day, and I can hear, even now, that old alarm clock ticking behind me. In the yard the boys were involved in play, but it was not their usual game of run and chase. They were beginning a game I had not witnessed before. I, of course, studied my charges, wondering what was afoot.

They drew lots. The winners were grouped as Southern Men. The losers were forced to play the part of Kansas Jayhawkers. As the game progressed, the Jayhawkers, led by a boy portraying the notorious John Brown, were routed by the Southern Men, Frank and Jesse among them, then chased into the brush. At last, the Southern Men captured the boy portraying John Brown, and he, without the slightest complaint, was led towards a tree in the yard.

"Hang John Brown," the boys chanted. "Hang John Brown from a sour apple tree."

One end of a rope was tied under the boy's arms and the other was tossed over the limb of the tree. As the boy was strung up, he contorted his face into a gruesome shape, mimicking the death throes of a man strangling. And it struck me that the boy being "hanged" must have actually witnessed such an event to have played his part in so convincing a manner.

John Brown's agonies increased and the Southern Men soon began cheering and singing songs. Horrified by the cold brutality of this spectacle, I cut recess short and went to the door.

"Come children," I called. "It's time for geography."

I was somewhat shaken in attempting to teach my lessons after that recess, but as the day progressed the children's horrible game passed from my mind. When the clock read noon, the children went outside with their lunch buckets, and I went to the window again, expecting that the boys would be involved in some more usual pastime. Darebase, an antecedent of our modern bat and ball games, was one of their favorites.

But again lots were drawn and the sides assembled. Another boy was chosen to play John Brown. Again he was captured and hanged to the cheers of the others. I suppose it's faulty memory that causes me to believe that all the children, boys and girls alike, were gathered around that tree when Brown was hanged this second time. At the very most, there were eight or ten of them watching, and the vision I now hold, of all seventy of my charges dancing and singing at the base of that tree, is something conjured in the more reptilian reaches of my soul.

In the following days, I assumed the children would tire of this game, but they did not. It became an obsession with them. At lunch, at every recess, they dashed to the yard and drew lots. It was cold and calculated and horrible. Every player knew their part down to the slightest gesture, and the game did not vary.

As the real violence going on along the border grew and the mock violence outside my schoolroom window continued, a sense of despair overcame me. It is well known that we were strong on the three R's in those days, but the school also functioned as an adjunct to church and family. We taught the children morality and their relation to society. Our McGuffy's Readers may seem almost humorous today, but they served to instill in generations the values which pervade our society even now.

Our Readers extolled the virtues of village life. They taught equality and egalitarianism. They taught that hard work would be rewarded and evil punished. Our Reader's lessons were filled with hope and an unwavering belief in man's progress and perfectibility.

The children read McGuffey and understood. The children believed that the hand of God could be seen in every act of man on earth, and there, in that weed-infested schoolyard, God's work was the hanging of John Brown.

Every day, I watched as the golden rule was twisted into some divine prescription for vengeance. Every day, I, a nomad, began thinking it might be wise to move on at the end of term. Yet, every time I resolved to give notice, McGuffey's admonition to "try, try again" prevented me.

I suppose it is nothing more than my own romanticism that causes me to believe I was clutching another book, more arcane than McGuffey, to my bosom on the day I arrived at my decision. Perhaps it was not "The Tell Tale Heart" or "The Masque of the Red Death" I was holding as I watched those children carry out their mock murders. But that old alarm clock was ticking behind me, I remember that, and John Brown's face was contorting in front of me.

"Hang John Brown," the children chanted. "Hang John Brown. Hang John Brown from a sour apple tree."

Then a child, unseen, came up behind me, and when she spoke I was so startled I dropped the book.

"Are you for slavery, Miss Helms?" the child asked.

Perhaps I was not even holding a book at the time. If I was, it would have been McGuffey not Poe. I doubt I would have brought Poe into the schoolroom for fear a member of the board might find it, but I had been reading his tales of tormented souls late at night, in bed, and when that child spoke all my cherished illusions about my duties as a teacher vanished.

"Are you 'slave,' Miss Helms, or are you 'free?'"

My own young mind was inundated by a vision of horror. These children were cursed. Death stalked the land. I lived in a schoolhouse in a secluded wood, and, above all, I was a woman and alone.

3

Summer 1858
Charlie Taney, Caretaker, Old Siloam Christian School
Excelsior Springs, Missouri

It was a bad afternoon, three years before the war. Hot, it was. The clouds were black, and the air had a weight to it—so wet it stuck to you like honey. Tornado weather, my pa used to say.

"You boys be careful, now," Frank's ma called out.

"Don't worry," Frank said.

We sat on two old horses in front of the James place. Fifteen years old, Frank and I were, almost military age, but still just barefoot farm boys.

Frank's ma said, "Where you goin', anyway?"

"Goin' swimmin'."

I admired Frank, in those days—tailed along behind him like a puppy dog—but what he'd told his mother was a lie. No good ever come from such a thing. We were "goin' swimmin'"—like he'd said—but not at the creek, like she must have figured. No sir, we had an idea to ride all the way to Fishing River—seven, eight mile as the crow flies.

"Be back 'fore supper," his ma ordered. "There's a storm blowin' up."

"Yes, Ma."

"And take Jesse with you."

"Oh, Ma."

Jesse was but eleven years of age, then, and his voice hadn't yet changed. He still sang in church, and I mean to tell you, us bullfrogs never wanted no sopranos tagging along.

"Not today, Ma."

"You do as I say, Mr. Frank."

Frank didn't savor it much, when his ma called him that, but we was afraid of his ma—everybody was— so he just reached down and pulled Jesse up on the horse behind him.

"Mr. Frank," Jesse said, just so.

"Choir boy," Frank shot back.

Nowadays, there's a town stands at Fishing River—got hotels and so on, restaurants and mineral baths. But when I was a boy-child it was God's own paradise there. Big elms on the bank. Mud cats, bass, bluegills so thick in the water, you could walk across 'em, like stones— "A river flows out of Eden..." Genesis, II, 10.

We was there, that stormy day, to investigate the mineral springs that bubbled up 'round there. My own baby cousin had been scrofulus until he'd drunk the miracle of the waters, and I'd bragged to Frank about it.

"Cures all," I'd said. "Scrofula. Sciatica. Rheumatis'."

"No such thing as miracle waters," he'd said—a doubter Frank James always was, and hell-bound, even then.

When we got there, to the river, he knelt right down in the mud, got it all on his trousers—didn't care none about that. Lifted a handful of this magic water up to his mouth. Smelled it. Licked at it with his tongue. Drank some, then spat it right out.

"Tastes poorly," he said.

"Ain't so bad," I told him. "You just prejudice. You just don't want nothin' to do with it. You just made up your mind and won't bend."

Jesse weren't that way. Jesse dashed right on up to the edge, flopped down, and dunked his whole front face in it. Sucked up a bellyful of the stuff then rolled on his back and spit it out like a fountain.

"No such thing as miracle water," Frank says.

"Mr. Frank," says Jesse, needlin' him.

Further up along the bank, we found this fat, old oak with roots so thick they heaved up the ground. Trunk was split in twain. Some boys before us had gone and tied a rope to one of the branches, and, the day was so hot, we had our clothes off in no time.

Took turns grabbin' the rope, swinging out and over the river, letting go and flying like fisherbirds. But Jesse, you see, he never was a patient boy, and, soon enough, he got bored with it all. Wasn't good enough for him, just swingin' on that rope, so he started braggin'. Bragged that he was going to fly out, over the river, touch his toes in mid-air, then dive head-first into the water.

"I got wings," says Jesse.

"But you ain't got the sand," says Frank.

Fool idea, it was. The water wasn't all so deep and you could get your neck broke doing what Jesse'd proposed. A boy from Bethany Plantation had dived head-first into the river, paralyzed himself, and died of it—or so the story went.

Jesse strutted round that fat, old tree, looking her up and down. He stretched out the swinging rope and measured it.

"All brag and no show," Frank said, but Jesse never backed down from nothin'.

He stepped back and made a little run at the rope. He clutched and grabbed and swung —as big a swing as a boy might hope. He flew off towards heaven. Started to touch at his toes but only got about halfway bent. Then he got all turned round in the air, mixed-up it seemed. He dangled there 'bout half a second, then straight down he went, like a sack of flour, slap on his back in the shallows.

Frank leaped right in after him, I'll give Frank that. Grabbed his little brother by the arm and pulled him up and out, rescued him—'cept he didn't need rescuing.

"You all right?"

"Leave me alone."

"Choir boy."

Jesse always had a temper, which is why he killed so many, I suppose. He stormed towards the bank. Set down by me in the grass. Drew his knees up into himself. Wrapped his arms around them.

"You all right?" I asked. "Ain't broke your courage or nothin'?"

"Shut up."

Frank said, "Charlie asked you a question. Don't you answer people's questions no more."

"Leave me alone."

Frank picked up a handful of mud and threw it at him. "Choir boy."

Jesse dodged it, so Frank just picked up another handful and, splat, this time the black mud hit square in Jesse's chest and splattered his face.

"The boy looks like a damn African," Frank said.

I laughed along. "Guess he does."

"Don't know how it could possibly be," Frank went on, "but my little brother seems to have African blood in him."

Jesse sneered. "Mr. Frank."

And that was when Frank blew up. He was mean, sometimes, and now the meanness was on him. He come after Jesse right off—charging out the water and up the bank. Jesse tried to dodge him, but Frank caught his scrawny, little leg. Pulled him down, hoisted him up, cradled him like a baby, and carried him back into the water.

"Are you washed in Jesus' blood?" Frank cried. "Are you washed in the blood of the atoning lamb?"

"Don't you dare!" Jesse said.

Frank spoke scripture. "'And the Holy Ghost descended in a bodily shape, like a dove upon him, and a voice came from heaven...'" Luke, III, 22.

I told Frank to stop, but he had a mean on, now, and he never paid me no mind, no way. He dunked Jesse down, like he was baptizing him. Two, three, four times.

"Mr. Frank! Mr. Frank! Mr. Frank!" Jesse came up kicking and spitting each time. Wouldn't give in.

The air was cracklin' electric from the storm by now, and big, fat rain drops had begun to fall—one, two, three—so slow you could count 'em. Frank dunked Jesse down again, but this time Jesse picked up a stone off the bottom. Round like an egg, it was—I saw it plain in his hand—round like an egg, but black, like iron.

The lightening flashed as he swung that smooth, old stone, and it come to me that the Lord would smite Frank and his blasphemy.

But the Lord did no such thing. Jesse swung and missed. Frank grabbed onto his wrist and held it firm. Bent it back, farther and farther, until Jesse let drop the stone. Then Frank pushed him under and held him down the longest time.

"You'll drown him," I called from the bank.

"He's only a damned choir boy," Frank said. But he let him up just the same.

The storm broke in earnest, then—"the same day were all the fountains of the great deep broken up, and the windows of the heavens were opened." Genesis VII, 11.

We rode home through the fury of it—the thunder like cannons, the lightening-flash. Three barefoot farm boys, lost in the wilderness—"And ye shall be as gods, knowing good from evil."

4
Autumn 1861
Billy Drury, Farmer
Clay County, Missouri

When the war started, I supposed I'd stay neutral—a foolish notion in retrospect. The problem being that it just wasn't one of your regular wars out here. No brass bands. No military balls. No parades or other such accouterments. Not even any front lines.

Out here, in the borderlands, it was guerrilla war—nighttime, shadow war, bloody and hate filled. Farms were burned and pillaged. Men were dragged from their beds and assassinated. Women were cast into prison and held without trial. Spies and informers were everywhere.

I was up on the roof one pleasant afternoon—an Indian summer day, it was—doing some needed repairs before the onset of winter. I was banging away with my little hammer, when the dogs, down in the yard, started barking. Fearing Redlegs, guerrillas, or just some fellows with guns, I stopped what I was doing, took a gander from my vantage point, and what should I see, come riding up the lane, but a big, old woman astride a big, old Missouri mule.

This seemed odd, if not threatening. But an ugly creature, she was, even at a distance —gray haired and bespectacled, with a big blue bonnet and a long checkered dress. Fat as a hog, she appeared to be, and, on her arm, she carried a splint basket filled with apples. Her legs were slung to either side of the horse, just like a man's, and when I saw that she was not only coming straight towards the house, but smoking a big cigar, besides, I decided to take action.

I scrambled down my ladder, went inside my humble abode, and possessed myself of the Colt Walker .44 that I'd procured around the same time martial law made such things illegal.

I kept this weapon greased and loaded, day and night. But I didn't keep it capped for fear it'd blow off and kill me, which meant I had to mount the percussion caps on the nipples now, with this strange creature coming up the lane and my fingers all a-tremble.

This done, I shoved the infernal device into my belt, said some prayers—as even us Freethinkers tend to do in times of peril—and stepped outdoors to greet my visitor.

"Afternoon," I said.

She commanded the mule to halt, "Ho, there," then held out her basket of apples and leaned down so I could examine the merchandise.

"Care to buy an apple, sir?"

Her voice seemed very odd, but I supposed the cigar accounted for that. Then, I looked again at her face, and it occurred to me that this supposed apple woman was in bad need of a razor and a shave.

"Coleman?" I said. "Thomas Coleman Younger?"

"None other," he laughed.

Later on, Coleman became the feared Cole Younger of the infamous James-Younger—or as Cole would prefer, the Younger-James—Gang. But he wasn't any famous outlaw in sixty-one. No sir, just another war happy, seventeen-year old was all he was.

"I need to ask your help, Mr. Drury," he said. Cole was like that, then, educated and polite—unlike most of our young men today.

27

"Why sure, Cole. I'm always ready to help a near neighbor. But what are the women's clothes for? Are you going to a masquerade ball of some sort?"

"Don't I wish," he laughed. "It's something like that, I suppose. A masquerade but with guns."

He pulled off his bonnet and gray wig and used them to rub the sweat and dirt off his face.

"Some bad men are after me," he said. "And I'm hungry. Can I ask you for something to eat?"

"Why sure. I got plenty. You just step on down and come on in."

That's when it all started, I realize now—outlaws using my place for a hideout. I didn't consider such a thing might happen at the time. Hadn't the slightest inkling of what Cole or Jesse or Frank would become. Cole was a good boy, you see—just like all of them—a young gentleman with a promising future. His father was one of the leading lights down in Harrisonville, and, like me, he'd sought to remain neutral in the war—at least until the Federals pillaged his livery stable.

"Your Uncle Benbow said you'd help," Coleman said, as he sat at my table, shoveling down beans and catfish.

I hadn't seen my uncle in some months, but it all made good sense. Cole's father owned farms all over, and one was near the Little Blue, in the Crackerneck region, where Uncle Benbow lived.

Cole looked up from his plate. "Your uncle hid me from the Federals. He said you were a loyal man."

"I'm as loyal as any man," I said, failing to add, that my first loyalty was to my little farm and my own skin.

"It started about a week ago," Cole began.

One of the Harrisonville ladies, he told me, had thrown a soiree of one sort or another, over to her place and some captain of the militia, the Federal militia, that is, had insulted Cole's sister at the dance. Cole, being young and excitable, took umbrage at whatever this captain had done, and the two of them fought. Cole won, and he'd supposed that would be the end of it, but the very next day, this captain, with all his men, came to Cole's house intent on gaining revenge.

"But, lucky for me, we got word he was coming," Cole said. "So I took to the brush. Been on the run ever since. Hidin' out. Stealin' apples and eatin' whatever I could. Starvin' mostly. Sick of apples... You know of a man called Quantrill?"

"Quantrill? No." I shook my head. The name didn't ring a bell, at the time, but it did later on—you can be sure of that.

"A little bird told me he's over near Rush Creek," Cole said. "I'm determined to join him and his Partisan Rangers."

"Why sure," I said, "you go and join your Rangers, if that's what you want. Every man must do what he thinks is right, I always say. And if there's anything I can do for you, you just let me know."

Now, I shouldn't ever have said that last part. It's just something people say when they're trying to be sociable, in my opinion, and nobody ever really supposes they'll get taken up on it. But take me up on it, Cole Younger did.

"I'll be needing to borrow your Walker Colt," he said, inclining his head towards my revolver, which lay, now, on a table near the door.

"That gun cost me a pretty penny, Cole."

"I'm sorry, Mr. Drury. But I need it more than you. Your Uncle Benbow gave me his shotgun, but I had to ditch it when I crossed at the Ferry. Wouldn't have looked right, an apple woman carrying a shotgun on the Ferry."

"No, suppose it wouldn't," I said.

He stood up, went to the table by the door, picked up the Colt, and inspected it.

"You'd probably just end up hurtin' yourself with a man-killer like this. I'll be doing you a favor by taking it off your hands."

He cocked that Colt like he meant business, and I always demur when a man cocks a Colt.

"Sure, Cole, sure," I said. "You take that gun if you want. You can slip a weapon like that right under your skirts, and no one will be any the wiser."

He shook his head. "I'm not going around like this anymore, you can be sure of that. I got my trousers and shirt on underneath, but, besides the Colt, I'll be needing a proper coat and a good hat."

"Well, I got a hat or two," I said. "But as far as coats are concerned, you're a few degrees larger than I."

"And I'll be needing your riding horse, too, Mr. Drury."

"My riding horse?" said I. "But that's Sam Patch. That horse is a thoroughbred and made to race."

I'd procured Sam some years before and named him after a certain daredevil who'd attained fame by jumping off of things. Buildings, cliffs, Niagara Falls—you name it, Sam Patch, the daredevil, would jump off it. Didn't survive the Niagara Falls attempt, if memory serves.

So the next morning, after breakfast, Cole mounted my beautiful Sam Patch, and set there atop him, carrying my revolver and wearing my best hat and coat—with the seams split out, I might add.

I gave Sam a last pat on the neck.

"Take good care of him," I said to Cole.

"That mule," Cole said, speaking of the animal he'd left me in exchange. "That mule belongs to Ross Effington down by Blue Springs. I'd surely appreciate it if you'd return him for me."

"Why sure, Cole. I'll just make it a point to ride him down to Blue Springs so's I can foot it back."

"Sorry, Mr. Drury," Cole said.

He bent over in the saddle, leaned down off Sam, reached out and offered his hand.

"I'll get your pistol back one day," he said. "This war can't last very long. And I'll get your Sam Patch back, too, and your coat besides."

"Why sure, Cole, sure. Of course you will."

I didn't concern much over losing the Colt Walker. Cole was right in that it was a foolish idea in the first place, me having a cannon like that. I doubt I would have had the nerve to blow a tunnel through a man even if I'd needed to, and the Yanks went hard on folks they caught with contraband.

But I do wonder, as I lie myself down to sleep, sometimes, whatever happened to poor, old Sam Patch. I'd raised him from a colt, you know. Frisky, he'd been in the spring of his youth—kicking up his hind legs and running in circles, just for the pure joy of it. I'd take him carrots and molasses, and he'd lick the molasses off my hand. Never once bit me, either.

Well, almost never.

I still can't forget the look in his eyes the day Cole rode off on him. Not understanding, but trusting, I think.

Shot dead, somewhere, in some goddamn ditch, I imagine.

"Goodbye," Cole cried, as he spurred my poor horse down the lane. "Goodbye and thank you."

"Goodbye." I waved. "Until I see you, Cole. God have mercy."

5

Autumn 1862
Merrill Corbett, Confederate Cavalryman
Letters to His Brother

Newtonia, Mo.
Sunday, Sept. 28
Dear Brother Robert,

My condition is much improved since my last writing as I can now be confident of having all the ink and paper required to correspond with greater frequency. I still do not trust the Office to get these letters through as I have not yet received the one you wrote on the occasion of my birthday. But at least I shall now have the wherewithal to scribble my lines when circumstance allows, and here, Dear Brother, is the story of this good fortune.

A week before we departed Arkansas, Sergeant Lamar came to me and said that Captain Brown, who is Colonel Keats' adjutant, wanted to see me.

"He needs a clerk," Lamar said, "and I recommended you."

Listen, Robert. Do not reveal such thoughts to Mother, but you know how bad I fared at the Elkhorn Tavern fight. If the fellows trouble me about having soft duty, then trouble me they will.

"Are you a man who can keep secrets?" Captain Brown asked me.

"As well as anyone," I said.

32

He is about twenty-three years of age and has a beard like a billy goat. I would not say he is frail, but that he is lacking in physique. His full name is Jason Alexander Xerxes Brown, but people call him "Jax."

"Sergeant Lamar tells me you know shorthand."

"I studied a book on it in school."

"He says you had two horses shot out from under you at Elkhorn Tavern."

"I did."

"How have your rations been?"

I shrugged. "Like everyone's."

At this, Brown called in his darky and had him get me some coffee with sugar mixed in and a dozen eggs. I didn't think I ought to let him buy me for a dozen eggs & some coffee, but buy me he did.

When I got back to our billet, Epps was making candles from some tallow he'd gotten hold of. He found it very amusing that I was going to be with Jax Brown.

"You'd be safer staying with us," he said.

I told him it would be well worth it if I could keep getting us eggs to improve our rations.

Epps just laughed. "Brown believes he can't be killed as long as he rides a sorrel horse, that's what Daniels says. He's crazy, like all of them. You'd be better off taking your chances with us privates."

I had heard this before, about Captain Jax Brown and the sorrel horses, but I hadn't thought much of it. Then, later, in the cold of the night, I got to remembering things and couldn't sleep.

One time past, Colonel Keats had us stage a mock battle for some Arkansas ladies down in Van Buren. They turned out in force to watch, and after the play was over, the officers held a jousting tournament. They fought with poles for lances, and devised helmets & shields for themselves, decorated in the most vivid colors. It was all madness.

Listen, Robert. After Elkhorn Tavern when the rifle balls were whining through the air and the reins were clipped from my hands, I knew I could not stand such a battle again. The horses fell from under us like leaves but screaming.

Tell Mother that I am safe and will take good care of myself. Kiss her for me, Robert.

Your Loving Brother,
Merrill N. Corbett

⌘

October 4
In Camp near Van Buren, Ark.
Dear Brother Robert,

You will see from the above, that we are already back in Arkansas, our tails between our legs. You have doubtless read of the Newtonia fight in the reports, and I am writing to assure you that I passed through without injury.

Tell Mother I hid behind a stone wall when the Yanks came and did not expose myself, which is, for the most part, true. They came out of a wood and advanced on our position, a mile over open ground, and were cut to pieces. I do not know how men can do such things.

When they turned to run, we of the cavalry pursued at the gallop and with a wild yell. Captain Brown, atop his magic sorrel, fought like a demon possessed. He is anything but frail when in battle & I fear Epps was right about the dangers of being in the company of him & Keats.

And here is a thing that disturbs me, Robert. Although the fight was scarce a week ago, it seems to me a dream, and not a real thing at all. It is more like something I read of in a book, which all makes for a curious feeling of melancholy.

Colonel Keats did not like retreating one bit.

"Just look at my iron men," he said, sad and watching, from atop a little hill.

The Yanks burned down his ropewalk, over at Keatsville, so he has something to fight about. But I am not so sure about the rest of us, and we are not made of iron, a thing Sidney Marion Keats would know if he had seen the surgeons at work.

I used to lament your Affliction, Robert, but now I envy you, as it will keep you from being marched into the Meat-Grinder with the rest of us. There is no jousting here, only artillery.

Yesterday, after his dictation, Brown detailed me and Corporal Daniels to buy him some peach brandy, which is plentiful around here.

But none of the citizens would take paper money from either side and we had to give them gold. When we fulfilled this Duty, Brown gave us each a bottle for our trouble and Epps & me & Fuller & Daniels held a jollification.

I know how Mother feels about strong drink, but things are different among us of the Damned. Tell her that the snows will be on us soon, and once we build our winter quarters, we will hibernate until the spring. Tell her I will have it soft as a result of being attached to Keats and Brown.

Your Brother,
Merrill N. Corbett

⌘

Sunday, November 16
Near Van Buren
Dearest Brother Robert,

I must extend my apologies for not having corresponded after my boast that I would write more. Although pen and ink are plentiful for me, I did not take into account how wordy Jax Brown can be, nor the result his wordiness would have on my poor, right hand.

Fuller had the flux of late, but assure Our Mother that all is well with me and that once the snows begin I will be safe.

A band of guerrillas under the infamous Quantrill came down and joined us some days ago, fresh off raiding in Kansas. One of them is a young man named Franklin James, from Clay near Kearney, related to the Novingers. When I heard this, I introduced myself, and told him I knew Tom.

"He rides with Howell's guerrillas, now," James laughed. "And I suppose he's doing fine, unless a ball has found him."

I am about fed up with that kind of bravado but said nothing.

This James is a colorful fellow, like all these guerrillas. He is a tall man who wears a red bandana around his head like a pirate. Like most of them, is dressed in a blue coat he took off a Yank. He is a strange

35

sort, at times warm, at others peculiar, but he seems decent enough. After we chatted a while, he said I seemed lonesome, which I didn't think showed so easy. He bought a bottle from Sergeant Lamar, which we drank.

Robert, you were so wise to take Our Mother to safety rather than remain in Clay. I knew things were bad at home, but James said Charlie Pick of Kearney—among others—was murdered by the Yanks, and that no one is safe.

As we drank our peach brandy I asked James how things were in Liberty, but he knew nothing of my darling Willa or her family. Later, I asked him if he would take a letter to her for me, if he ever went north again.

"Pretty soon you can take it to her yourself," James said.

When I asked him how such a thing could be, he seemed taken back that I hadn't heard about "the invasion."

"What invasion is that?"

"Why, of Missouri, of course."

"But the Yanks settled our hash at Newtonia."

"Newtonia," James laughed. "Why, don't you see? Your little retrograde movement has just lured them all the farther south. Nothing else but invasion is spoken of among the men of Quantrill."

I took this up later with Epps, and he said he had heard all about it, and it seems we are about to go warring again. What surprises me as odd is that Jax Brown never said nothing to me about this, and I am beginning to wonder if he suspects my loyalty.

Your Brother,
Merrill N. Corbett

⌘

Monday, December 1
My Dear Brother Robert,

We run into the Federals just a few miles north and our so-called invasion got cut short. I pray that this is the end of it, and that the snows will begin, but I am not certain of anything anymore. I did my

Duty, and you can assure Our Mother that once more I came through the scrape untouched by harm.

During the fight, I saw Franklin James of Clay charge forward as if in madness—his red bandana wrapped round his head, a pistol in each hand, and the bridle reins clenched in his teeth. He threw his very life at the Yanks as if it was nothing, and I think there is some kind of battle madness that infects them all. Sometimes, I feel it, too, and, despite my fears, I charge off with Brown and Keats intent on winning the day or dying.

I took down a report to Marmaduke in which Captain Brown said our casualties were light, but I told him I did not believe it.

"If you've turned coward," he said, "I can put you in Quartermasters."

I told him I didn't like the idea of dying, but that I was prepared to do the Honorable thing. He was pleased with my words, but I was too embarrassed to repeat them to Epps.

Among the wounded was George S. Fuller, a young man from home, who had been very nice to me. He took a ball in the hip and so passed into the clutches of the surgeons. Epps and I went looking for him today amongst the buckets of arms and legs, but no one knew a thing about him, or even if he was alive or dead.

After that we got very drunk, and Epps said he had seen our own men robbing the bodies of their dead comrades for trousers and shoes. Then, after a long silence, he brought up the possibility of the two of us making a run for it.

"I don't think I could live with myself if I did that," I told him.

"You're as crazy as Franklin James," Epps said.

Tell Mother nothing.

Your Loving Brother,
Merrill N. Corbett

⌘

Prairie Grove, Ark.
Monday, December 7
Dearest Brother Robert,

Much has happened and there is little time to tell it. I have found a dry place with Brown, but it is cold, and the enemy is near.

A few days ago, we cooked five days rations, and moved up the Fayetteville Road. The ladies all turned out to see us, and the old men waved. The bands played, and the little boys ran alongside our shabby columns. It was all very stirring, but we are without wagons or tents.

The first night Epps and I huddled in the cold. The side of me facing the fire was hot, but the rest of me froze, so I had to keep turning myself like roast on a spit.

"With all the stragglers," Epps said. "No one would notice if we slipped away."

"Brown would notice," I said. "And more, they'd send the guerrillas after us."

Epps nodded his head but avoided my eyes. He got into a scrape with Franklin James, the day before, and, I tell you, I do not think I would like it much if this James "took umbrage" with something I had said.

At dawn, there was frost on the ground, and we thought our misery could get no worse, but the rain started coming down in buckets. We rode north, dripping wet all day long, and I could not stop thinking about dying in the mud and muck.

Late in the afternoon, it started to snow, and not long after, Epps disappeared.

Today, Colonel Keats, Jax Brown, myself and some others were almost captured. We were on the Fayetteville Road, taking possession of a number of enemy wagons, when a whole company of Yanks appeared. They surrounded us, and we were overwhelmed so quickly that nothing could be done. When a Yank captain offered terms, Captain Brown objected, but Keats said we had no choice.

"We ought to die where we stand," Brown said, but Keats was adamant.

When we surrendered, I admit I was pleased by it all, and even jovial, though I tried to hide it. Despite knowing that capture meant prison and all the more suffering, the most awesome sense of peace overcame me. But not an instant after the Yanks got us, some of Quantrill's men appeared, in their blue coats and wild garb.

I shall not forget the sight, Franklin James in his mad, pirate bandana, thundering down upon us. Wild riders, these guerrillas are, a specter of Fury and Death in the charge.

"God bless those boys," Keats cried, swinging his big hat.

Once the rescue was effected, Captain Brown shook the hand of every man among them. Keats, grinning like a fool, was almost comical when he embraced the lanky James. For a moment, I thought he was going to kiss his cheeks like the Frenchies do.

"Sir, you have saved our lives and fortunes, our all. We owe you everything."

James was at a loss to reply, but muttered something about Duty. He's a stiff fellow, as I said, and he has tombstones in his eyes.

I have asked James to take a letter to my Darling Willa for me. He will be back up in Clay before I ever am, and, for all his faults, there is no one I would trust more with such a thing.

"You'll be able to take it yourself, before long," he said, when I first tried to give him the letter.

"I would much appreciate it, sir."

We stood without speaking for an instant, the letter in my fingers, dangling between us. Then, he removed his glove and took it.

"I'll make sure your girl knows how brave you were," he said. "She'll know what you gave for your country. None will ever forget."

He shook my hand and seemed quite moved. There was a tear in his eye, and I now feel somewhat sheepish in having thought him dead inside. But that is the key to it, I think, this battle madness that inflicts a man, being already dead inside and giving yourself up to it.

Robert, I am prepared to do my Duty, and when this awful war ends you must go see My Darling for me. You must tell her how I loved her, and that our love is all I have left that stands opposed to Death. Kiss Mother. Kiss Willa. One day, we shall all be together again.

Your Loving Brother,
Merrill N. Corbett

6

Spring 1863
Rudy Schaffer, Storekeeper
Liberty, Missouri

All the old timers around here can tell you a story or two about Jesse James. How they arm-wrestled him. How he out shot them at a turkey shoot. How he paid their mortgage.

I was about two years old when Jesse was assassinated, so I don't have any stories of my own. But my grandfather—August Groh, my mother's father—used to claim that he was the first man ever robbed by Frank James. He lived his last few years down at the Odd Fellows Home, and I heard the story so many times, I can tell it better than even he could.

When I was a boy, he used to tell it every Thanksgiving and Christmas, every Fourth of July and Decoration Day. Every time the family got together, Grandpa August would drag out his old Frank James story.

A German immigrant and self-made, Grandpa was, and there's nothing more American, I'd say, than a self-made immigrant. He did quite well during the war selling crackers— hard tack, that is—to the Federals. He had something to do with the commissary department, though I don't know what. He turned those crackers into a fortune, and was so proud of them that, after the war, he kept a couple of barrels full as souvenirs.

He used to bring a few crackers out at Thanksgiving—they keep forever, you know—and make us children see if we could figure out a way to eat them without breaking a tooth. You had to soak 'em first, in coffee or something, to soften them up—or maybe fry 'em in fat. Awful things, they were.

It happened, once, during the war, that Grandpa August had to go from Liberty to Kansas City on some sort of business involving these crackers. He'd gotten a pass from the Provost Marshal to travel—they were under martial law in those days. But, for some reason, he was unable to arrange transport on a public conveyance and, his business being urgent, he decided to ride all the way to Kansas City on a horse.

He had a beautiful, old house on the outskirts of town, when I was a boy. He bought it right after the war when prices were dirt cheap. It had been a farm or plantation of some sort before that, but he sold off most of the land and just kept the main house.

Out back there was a big maze made out of hedges—eight feet high. He'd tell us children that Jesse James' treasure was buried inside that maze, and we'd go out there and play for hours. We'd get lost, inside, you see—a good way for the adults to get some peace, I later learned. Sharp as a tack, Grandpa August was.

He'd lean back in his chair after Easter dinner and loosen his belt—which embarrassed my mother. Then he'd slap his big, old tummy—which embarrassed her even more.

"Ja, ja," he'd say, with a big grin. "Once I got robbed by Frank James."

He had something of an accent, but not too stilted. Self-educated besides being self-made. Learned the language all on his own. Came from somewhere over in Germany—Wurtemberg, I believe it was called—around the time of the California gold rush.

But Grandpa August wasn't about to scratch in the dirt for his fortune, no sir. He had an uncle in Philadelphia, Rudy Grutze, his name was—I'm named after him—so that was where he first went. Grandpa, being a smart fellow, got his Uncle Rudy to lend him some money which Grandpa used to buy pistols. He filled up two valises with pistols, then came out to St. Jo, which was the jumping off point for the Far West in those days. He sold those pistols for a big profit and, with the proceeds, set himself up in the grocery business.

"Yes, yes," Grandpa would say. "I remember it good. I was riding out from Liberty to K.C. On horseback of all things." He'd shake his head and laugh.

"I weren't so fat back then."

The whole table—my sisters and brothers, aunts, uncles, cousins, everyone -- would fall silent. We all knew that, sooner or later, we'd have to listen to Grandpa's tale about Frank James so we'd just pipe down and eat our chicken and dumplings and let him get on with it.

Grandpa was on his horse, and he had a military pass. The country around here was dangerous during the war, but he didn't apprehend any trouble. There hadn't been but a smattering of guerrilla activity since the previous fall, and, besides that, the roads were patrolled by Federals.

So there he was, just riding along, and, about noon, he came to this big stand of sycamores just the other side of Mill Creek. And, what do you think? Out of the brush come four men on horseback, brandishing pistols.

"Stand and deliver!" one of them cried.

A tall fellow, this one was, with black hair that curled down around his shoulders. Arthur Howell, he turned out to be—"Bub" Howell—about as cruel a guerrilla as ever lived.

Grandpa didn't realize who he was, at the time. But since they were all pretty tawdry looking, and, since they were all dressed in blue coats, his first impression was that they were Federals and maybe even deserters.

"Get down off that animal, sir," Bub Howell commanded.

Grandpa complied, but he didn't crawl. No, he was clear about that. He dismounted his horse, prepared to give these fellows whatever they asked, but determined to die dignified if it came to that.

Howell told one of his men, "Get to work and see what the son of a bitch has got."

With that, another fellow—also tall and lanky—got down off his horse and demanded that Grandpa August empty his pockets. Grandpa did this, even though it pained him—one hundred twenty-five dollars, and in gold, he had on him.

"Give it up," this second fellow commanded, and that was when Grandpa recognized him.

"Mr. Franklin James? Is that you there?"

As I said, Grandpa had been very successful in the grocery business. Besides having a store in Liberty, he had another up in Kearney, Jesse's hometown and, as the Jameses had patronized it for years, he'd gotten to know them all by sight.

"What in heaven are you doing robbing peoples in the road like such a common criminal? And what would your mama say about such goings on?"

"Don't talk so much," James told him.

"Have you deserted the army?" Grandpa asked, still thinking they were Federals. "How could you have stooped so low, Franklin? Your mama must be much ashamed."

"I'm a Southern soldier fighting for my rights, and I have my mother's blessing."

"God in heaven, what rights do you get for yourself in robbing poor travelers? What kind of rights is that?"

"You hardly seem poor, sir." Frank had Grandpa's gold coins, by now, along with his pocket watch. "You have gold. You have a pass from the military police, and I suspect, sir, that you are a profiteer and a poltroon."

"You talk nonsense." Grandpa shook his finger at Frank. "I just try to make a living, and I'm going to tell your mama about this the next time I see her."

"You just go ahead and do that," James said. "But first, take off your boots."

"My boots? You ain't going to take my boots?"

"I need a new pair of boots," Frank said. "And it looks like my feet will go into your boots nicely enough."

"How do you expect I should ride without boots?"

The curly haired one, Bub Howell, still up on his horse, laughed at that.

"You won't have anything to ride, you stupid fool. We're taking your horse, if you haven't figured that out yet."

"My horse?"

"Shut up and take off your boots or I'll kill you where you stand."

Bub Howell leveled a big pistol at Grandpa August, and, at long last, he realized the trouble he was in.

A great old man, Grandpa was. I remember one time when we were all picnicking down at Shoal Creek, and we children had to stop our play and gather around and listen, one more time, to that old story about Frank James.

"So I took the boots off, and what do you think? Yes? I took the boots off and said, 'You are welcome to them, sir.' Stupid man I was. You know? Going to die dignified. Hah. So, yes, I gave them the boots. I gave them the gold. I gave them the pass and my watch and even my pocket knife."

"And what do you think? I started walking back to Liberty, barefoot no less, and a Federal patrol arrested me for not having a pass. I tells them 'Franklin James has stolen it,' but they didn't believe me. Kept me two days in jail with a hundred others, until they gets it right."

He'd laugh a good, old laugh at that. First man ever robbed by Frank James, that's some distinction, I'd say.

A family joke, it got to be. Grandpa would be setting on the swing on the porch, in the warm evening on the Fourth of July, when we children would be dying to set off our firecrackers and pinwheels and Roman candles.

"Things was best in the old days," he'd say. "Ja, ja."

And we were stuck with it again—listening to how he was robbed by Franklin James.

I guess I've told that story almost as many times as Grandpa August did. I tell it to the children. I tell it to my customers—hope I don't drive too many of them away. As bad as old Grandpa August, I've gotten to be.

7

Summer 1863
Arthur 'Bub' Howell, Partisan Ranger
Letter to The Concord Tribune

Mr. Editors,

The absurd policies of Ewing have again brought about the murder of innocents. He has imprisoned our women without charge and only because they were the wives and mothers of patriotic men. He threw them in a dark jail in Kansas City and were that not enough, he brought about a so-called accident in which my own sisters and a half dozen other of these ladies were crushed to death and a dozen more horribly crippled to never be the same again.

And this is not the end of it.

Just last month there entered my band a young man named Jesse James from Clay. He is a boy not sixteen years of age, and what do the Federals do to such innocents?

Captain Bowers and his so-called militia came to this boy's farm to extort information for the reason that they suspected his brother of being a Southern man and with Quantrill. They chased down the boy aforementioned as he ran through the tall corn then lashed his bare back until he lay helpless. The scars make a gruesome sight.

Once this hideous deed was done, they strung up the boy's stepfather by the neck. They pulled him up slow and let him kick. When he was choked and half unconscious they lowered him back down and questioned him. When he would still not answer their demands, they raised him up again. And this they did six times more, stringing him up then letting him down, while all the while his weeping wife, heavy with child, pleaded for mercy.

And how did these jackals reward so brave a woman? I will tell you. They threw her into a dungeon and left her there to rot.

The sum total of all the horrors committed against us is too numerous to mention, but every fair minded man is well aware of them. It is bad enough that Jim Lane and his Redlegs drive us from our homes and burn and loot, but to make war against women and children is beyond all comprehension.

My only joy in this hell we call Missouri is that by doing such acts the Federals only seal their own Doom. Every time they whip a boy like J. James they make a man who will stop at nothing until he sees their destruction, and that is my only desire in this life and the next.

People of Concord, say this to Captain Bowers and his hirelings— Our Ladies must be Released. This is no idle threat. If they are not let go by three days from receipt of this letter I will capture some Concord ladies and do my worst. After that I shall go to Lawrence and find Jim Lane and bring him into the public square and hack off his head with a rusty saber.

Do not think I am jesting in this. God says it is an eye for an eye and a tooth for a tooth, and if Anarchy reigns then it is the fault of Bowers and Lane and Ewing, not Bub Howell.

Yours Respectfully,
A. G. Howell, Capt.
First Mo. Guerrillas

8
August 1863
THE NEW YORK EMPIRIC

THE ATTACK ON KANSAS
—✶—

Details Concerning the Sack of Lawrence
Citizens Killed Without Mercy
The Heroic Acts of Women
Senator Lane Unharmed

At dawn, yesterday morning, the guerrilla chief Quantrill led five hundred raiders into the town of Lawrence, Kansas, and commenced to burn, pillage, and kill with a ferocity unmatched in the long and bloody history of warfare along the border.

For two days, the raiders advanced in secret upon the doomed town, pressing farmers into service as guides, then killing them when their usefulness was at an end. When, at last, they reached the outskirts of the place they let out a rebel yell and charged up the main street firing their pistols into businesses and homes without distinction. They terrorized the town for three long hours, looting banks, stores, and saloons. They burned everything in their path, and murdered at least one hundred fifty innocents.

Your correspondent has witnessed scenes of brutality and horror on the battlefields of this long and terrible war, but here, at Lawrence, there was cold-blooded murder and nothing more. Men were murdered. Boys were murdered. Leading citizens of the town were shot down before the eyes of their families.

James Fitzgerald was forced to bring the rebels water and was shot dead for his trouble. In the Reliance Store, James Beard and P. W. Smalley, clerks, gave the rebels all their money, complied with all their requests, and were still shot down.

Certain Union officers, staying at the Westlake Hotel, came outside and surrendered, then were lined up against a wall and robbed. They begged for their lives, but the guerrilla captain Bub Howell ordered them killed.

A man named Alexander, a blacksmith by trade, grabbed his baby boy and hid in the corn, near town. But when the baby's cries gave him away, Alexander was discovered and murdered. His dead body was found still clutching the crying babe.

Judge Dawes was wounded in his yard and fell. His wife threw herself upon his body and begged for mercy, but the rebels dismounted, pulled her away from her fallen husband, and killed him with a shot to the temple. Mrs. Sarah White put out fires kindled to burn her house, thereby saving her husband who was hidden under the floor. Mrs. Wilhemina Heitmuller directed certain men the guerrillas were hunting into a large storm cellar near the center of town and hid them there.

One of Quantrill's lieutenants, a man named Younger, was, himself, so revolted by the carnage that he rode down the main street beseeching people to run for their lives.

Now, Lawrence is a mass of smoldering ruins. The bereaved and homeless are everywhere. Women and children weep in the barren streets. Men rake through the ruins of their homes, searching for any lost treasure that may give them comfort. The air is so permeated by ash that a breath cannot be drawn without choking.

James H. Lane, the famed Kansan of the Border Wars and long-time enemy of Quantrill, was among those men the bushwhackers were hunting. It was feared, at first, that he had fallen into their hands, but we can now give thanks for it has been learned that he is, instead, leading an expedition to Missouri in pursuit of the guerrillas.

We have learned that General Ewing, commanding the military district, intends to issue an order that will deny the guerrillas the aid and sustenance given them by the traitors residing in the border counties of Missouri. Within a few days, he will order that all people residing in Bates, Cass, Jackson, and Vernon counties remove themselves at once from their present places of residence. Those who can prove their loyalty to the Union will be given certificates and allowed to take up residence at military stations. Others will be removed by force of arms if necessary.

This order will depopulate a strip of land some thirty miles wide. It is a form of warfare we detest, but it is the rebels who began this war, and we who must finish it.

We give below a list of the white men murdered at Lawrence. No women or children were harmed. A number of Negroes were also killed, but we did not get their names.

9

October 1863
Julia Fanning Breckenridge, Housewife
Montgomery, Alabama

I was raised in Monrovia, Missouri—a sleepy river village of white houses and brick buildings, an idyllic setting of the type that has not survived into the new century. Before the war, my people were numbered among the most substantial in the county—my father being owner and proprietor of the ferry at Monrovia and also its largest warehouse.

But the war, as you might imagine, changed all that. Even though Monrovia was well north of the regular lines, my father's holdings were plundered by Yankees on more than one occasion. For a time we were protected from such marauders by Captain Arthur Howell and his Partisan Rangers. And it was while the Captain made his headquarters in Monrovia that I became acquainted with Jesse James.

I do not recall the year in which the incident I am about to describe occurred, but I can tell you it must have happened on a Friday night in October. We were putting up apple butter, you see, and we always prepared the apples for cooking on a Friday night in October.

The whole family—with the exception of my father who was serving with Sidney Marion Keats—was gathered in the kitchen. The smell of hot cider filled the air. Baskets filled with apples were piled everywhere. My sisters and I cored them as fast as we could, while mother cranked the old apple peeler.

My grandmother was still alive, then, though quite old and wizened. Her corncob pipe and rude table manners betrayed a frontier upbringing. She was arthritic and deaf, besides, and yet it was she, that night, who first heard the beat of horses hooves.

"Lord God. Soldiers."

In an instant my mother was at the window. She pushed back the curtains as much as she dared and peered down the dark lane that ran past our house. My sisters and I sat frozen in fear, but when mother turned to us smiling, we knew all was well.

"It's Bub Howell's boys," she said, "and one of them," she looked at me, "is pulling up right outside."

My sisters giggled. My mother hushed them.

"Now be quiet girls," she said with a smile. "You know how agitated Julia is these days."

I assumed as haughty an air as I could manage at age sixteen. "I don't care a whit about Mr. Jesse James."

At the time I despised, or thought I despised, the handsome, young Ranger. He came around whenever Captain Howell's company was in Monrovia but seemed to exhibit an interest in every member of the family but me. For my part, I tried to ignore him. It was only years later, in reflecting back on our immaturity and inexperience, that I was able to understand the true nature of our feelings.

"Mrs. Fanning," Jesse said, as my mother showed him in.

"Miss Julia," he said to me. Coolly, I thought.

"Mr. James," I replied, pretending to be hard at work on an apple.

Jesse was a mere boy, himself, I now realize. His uniform, so-called, was nothing more than odds and ends he had been able to gather. He was covered from head to foot with the dust of the road, but to me he seemed the epitome of the gallant soldier, a dashing cavalier upholding the righteous cause of the South.

My mother set a chair for him, between me and my grandmother, and shoved a plate of gingerbread into his hands.

He ate with a hunger he could scarcely conceal, but before I could think of even a single thing to say, my little brother was on him, begging to play with one of the two big revolvers that were thrust in his belt.

"You're too little for such things," Jesse said, brushing the child's hands away. Then he smiled and pointed at the guns in turn. "This one, here, I call Beauty. This other one, here, I call Beast."

My little brother touched a delicate finger to a big knife that hung in a scabbard on Jesse's waist.

"What's that one named?"

Jesse shook his head and laughed. "Don't you know nothin'? You don't name knives, just guns and horses."

My grandmother lit that awful pipe of hers. "Kilt any Yankees?"

Jesse patted Beauty. "I killed a fellow that was a chaplain with this one. Guess I'll pay for that, one day, if what the Bible says is true. But for now we must live by the law of the tooth and fang, that's what Captain Howell says."

My grandmother persisted. "How many you kilt all told, boy?"

Jesse thought for a moment. "Why, seven I can count for sure."

"Seven!" Granny laughed, taking his statement for an idle boast. "Why, you ain't been in the army long enough to have killed seven men."

"It's true," Jesse said. "Captain Howell says I'm the keenest fighter he's got, and I can prove it."

He begged to be excused and, this granted, he proceeded out the door and into the yard. We all waited in bewilderment until, a few moments later, Jesse returned with the throat latch of his horse's bridle.

"See here. See 'em Julia." He passed the horrible thing right under my nose.

"Well, by God," my grandmother exclaimed "One, two, three -- well, by God, yes. There are seven scalps there."

My grandmother was no stranger to the cruel nature of guerrilla warfare. In her day the enemy had been the Mormons, and she was used to such atrocities. But to me the "trophies" Jesse laid before us seemed to putrefy the very air.

"See, Julia. That one there is the chaplain's."

Blood rushed towards the top of my head, and I felt, for a moment, as if it might explode out my skull.

"You are not a gentleman, sir, but a murderer and a savage. You may live by the law of the tooth and fang, but we are civilized people, and if you persist in acting like a beast, you are welcome to leave."

"Julia Fanning!" my mother exclaimed. "Mr. James is your guest. You apologize this minute!"

But it was too late for such civilized sentiments. The shy, handsome boy who had killed seven men in battle cowered before me like a cat that had been doused with a bucket of water. It seemed that he wanted to speak, but when words failed him, he bolted for the door.

"Mr. James." My mother chased after him, but failing in that, she turned and began to scold me for my behavior.

"Julia Fanning. What has gotten into you?"

Already I had begun to regret my hasty words. I thought to chase after him, too, but before I could a pistol shot exploded in the yard. I jumped with fright and froze. We all fell silent and listened.

Then, we heard the shout of a single word.

"Hypocrites." And Jesse James was gone.

Now, I deeply regret what I said to the young volunteer that night. Had normality and peace been the order of the day I imagine Jesse would have tried to impress me with his prowess as a ballplayer or wrestler. Perhaps he would have tossed rocks at me and my sisters as we walked home from school. Instead, all he could do was show me those horrid scalp locks for which, in his own soul, he must have paid a price beyond imagining.

A few days later a column of Yankees under Captain Bowers moved on Monrovia with the intent of capturing or killing Arthur Howell and destroying his command. But it was Bowers, instead, who was ambushed and destroyed on a narrow, tree-shaded lane that ran not far from our home.

Jesse James fought with great ferocity in that action, I understand, but did not take a single scalp. I have been told, in fact, that after that Friday, when we were putting up apple butter, he never scalped another man. I do not know if that is true or not. I do know, however, that he never came calling again.

10

March 1864
Darla Starr, Proprietor, Darla's Salon de Joie
Ft. Smith, Arkansas

My mother crept down the back stairs of her father's place. She was quiet. She was careful. She was sixteen years old and in love. A fat, Texas moon lit her way across the yard. Her lover was waiting by the barn—Cole Younger, nineteen and dashing, blue eyed and fair.

"Belle. Over here."

Her favorite mare stood saddled by the gate—so shining black it was blue in the moonlight. She swung into the saddle like a man—quick and easy, unafraid. She wore a velvet riding habit and a cowboy's hat pinned back at the brow—the Belle Starr of legend, bold and daring, flamboyant.

There came a shout from the house—her father.

"Belle, damn you. Get back here!" He had his old ten gauge.

"Goodbye," she called, laughing.

"Let's go," Cole said, seeing the gun.

Frank James and Tom Novinger met them in some cottonwoods where a stream crossed the road. They fell in behind, pulled out their pistols, fired into the black sky, and yelled their rebel yells.

"Ei-yah. Ei-yah."

They flew across the open prairie. There were still buffalo and wild horses, then. Cole pulled his pistol, grinned at Belle, and fired a shot at the Milky Way. The horses were lathered and dripping, their big hearts pumped.

She had a power over men, my mother did—even at sixteen. She wasn't pretty but determined and striking. Her hair was as black as a crow, and her eyes were as black as her hair.

She came from Carthage, Missouri, originally, where her father kept a livery stable and a tavern for travelers. She'd graduated the Female Academy there, where she'd learned piano and Latin, needlepoint and manners. But when the war came, her brother joined the guerrillas and everything changed.

Carthage got burned to the ground, and the family fled to Texas, like thousands of other refugees—all the goddamn way to Texas in a covered wagon, if you can imagine such a thing. They settled just east of Dallas, in a town called Solo, where my grandfather, my mother's father, established a tavern on the highway to Shreveport. Solo wasn't much, just a wide bend in the road—a store, a saloon, and the tavern—a mud hole in winter and a dust bowl in summer.

Her father wouldn't let her go anywhere or do anything, and it drove my mother wild. But that winter, Quantrill and his guerrillas came south, like flying birds, and in December, on New Year's Eve, Cole Younger walked into Solo Tavern.

My mother and my grandmother had been cooking all day, getting ready for the evening's celebration. They'd laid out quite a spread in the Common Room downstairs where travelers ate and slept. My mother was carrying in a platter of sweet 'taters when their eyes first met.

Imagine that, laying eyes on the love of your life, when you're carrying in sweet 'taters.

Later, she played the piano for him—Chopin, or something like it. They sat on the piano bench, side by side. Everyone else bundled up and went outside for the fireworks, but Cole and Belle lingered. He'd been one of the raiders who'd sacked Lawrence, Kansas, a few months before, and the horror of it troubled him.

"I didn't get into this war to kill innocents." He shook his head. "I didn't become a soldier just to become a murderer."

My mother told him how the Yankees killed her brother.

"I want to get the bastards," she said.

It wasn't proper language for a woman, but that was my mother, and bold men liked her for it. Cole smiled and put his arm around her—you know what he was after.

"I'll get them for you," he told her.

"I want to get them myself," she said.

When the fire crackers started popping off in the yard, they went outside. The rockets flew off on a whoosh of flame, and someone had dug a hole in the hard dirt and filled it with gunpowder. When they touched it off, the damn thing near blew the house down.

"Son of a bitch," Cole laughed.

"I love it," Belle said.

Later, there was dancing—waltzes and mazurkas—and they danced the Virginia Reel—Cole Younger, my father, and Belle Starr, my mother. She was so set on him, she wouldn't accept any other partners that night, and that made her father suspicious.

"You're too damn young for a man like that," he told her. "God knows where he's been. God knows what he's seen and done."

"I've seen all he's seen," my mother said. "Look how they killed poor Tommy. Look what they did to Carthage. Who I see is none of your goddamn business."

"Don't you talk to me like that, young lady."

Later, that night, he locked her in a closet to keep her away from him.

"You're not growing up a whore if I can help it."

Now, they galloped towards the river—Belle and Cole, Frank James and Tom Novinger—whooping and laughing, shooting at the moon and even hitting it, if what my mother used to say is true.

Near White Rock Creek, at the Clement Farm, the wedding party met their guests—a troop of cavalry, the best the Confederacy could muster. Not Quantrill or Bub Howell and his murderers, but Major Jax Brown and Captain Dick Sturgis—Sidney Marion Keats' men—all in their best uniforms, all bright and cheering as Cole and Belle rode up.

They had a preacher in tow, a Methodist they'd kidnapped from the log church in the grove. He was mounted on a mule, half dressed, shivering, and not very happy.

"This is an outrage," he told Major Brown. "And it is no proper way to have a wedding. The girl is too young, and I refuse to be a party to marrying her off."

"If you won't do it," Jax Brown said, "I will."

"You're not empowered to do any such thing."

Jax Brown drew his pistol. "If a ship's captain can marry people, then a major in the service of the Confederacy ought to be able to. Just give me your book and show me the words."

The preacher relented, and Major Brown called his men to attention. They drew their sabers and snapped to—rigid and handsome in their saddles. Frank James dismounted and held my mother's horse. Tom Novinger held my father's, and there, under a silver moon, on the Texas prairie at midnight, Belle Starr and Cole Younger became man and wife.

For pure romance, it's a story that can't be beaten. But life isn't always like a story, and the ending of this one wasn't so perfect. About a month after that moonlight wedding, my father ran off to play war again. He left my mother in the lurch, and the son of a bitch didn't come back until four years later, on the run from the law, and begging her to hide him.

Cole Younger had enough courage to fight a war, ride with Jesse James, and rob banks and trains, but he was too goddamn big a coward to raise his own baby daughter. I've written him and gone to see him, but he won't have any part of me. He says I'm not his. He says I just want money, but that's ridiculous. I've made more money in my business than he ever stole in his. I don't want money. I want a father.

My mother robbed stagecoaches and dealt Faro, ran with outlaws and trafficked in stole horses. She had more husbands and lovers than I can count on fingers and toes put together. All she ever did for me was shunt me from pillar to post and lock me up in boarding schools—just like her father locked her in that closet.

"I want you to grow up right," she'd tell me. "I don't want you to end up like your mama. Understand?"

She ended up shot dead in the road near Eufala, Oklahoma, and I ended up a whore, dying from the inside out. I don't want that to happen to my daughter, so I give her everything. The best schools. Piano lessons. Dramatics. The best is what my daughter gets. She won't end up like me.

11

October 1864

THE NEW YORK EMPIRIC

THE MISSOURI GUERRILLAS STRIKE

—*—

The Heartless Butcheries of Howell
A Guerrilla Shows Mercy

Information received confirms that the notorious Arthur "Bub" Howell attacked the town of Concord, Missouri, yesterday, captured an entire train, set fire to a number of buildings, and murdered seven unarmed civilians.

Howell and his band, numbering some seventy-five bushwhackers, all dressed in Union coats, descended on the unsuspecting town at about eleven o'clock in the morning. The church bells rang out their warnings, but too late, for the vermin had already infested the once clean and peaceful streets.

Howell and six of his men struck the four-horse stage from Corinth, shot the driver dead, and ordered the passengers into the road. Howell singled out Mrs. Garnetta Peyton of Concord and her Negro servant, a harmless, white-haired, old man.

"What are you doing riding in the coach with your mistress? You should ride on top with the rest of the baggage."

"I'm a free man, sir," the old Negro replied.

"What did you call me? You call me master if you call me anything."

Howell declared that he would shoot the both of them, but at that moment, the passenger train from St. Louis was heard steaming towards the station and the bushwhackers rode off after bigger game.

The train and depot were captured, robbed, and set afire, then the Concord Female Academy was attacked. The girls were ordered into the yard, but just as Howell's men were making ready to put the building to the torch, two of the girls shouted out that they were all rebels and, when Howell's men were convinced of this, the building was spared.

Stores were looted and burned. The courthouse was set aflame in an attempt to destroy all records and deeds contained therein. The homes of loyal Union men were singled out and attacked. John Miller was shot dead for the crime of having an American flag in his house. Elmer Burchart, Monte Waller, and Joseph Roland were also murdered.

Adair Cheney, who has a large farm just outside the town, was dragged from his hiding place in a root cellar. He was taken to the kitchen where Howell's men were molesting his servants and Howell, who had by this time, broken into the liquor cabinet, ordered Cheney lashed to a chair.

"Where is your money hidden?" he demanded.

"I have no money," Cheney declared. "The war has taken it all."

"You're lying," Howell said. "You made plenty of money off your niggers before you freed them."

He thrust his revolver into Mr. Cheney's ear and threatened him with death. Then, Mrs. Iona Drake Cheney, came into the kitchen.

"What on earth are you doing?" the brave woman said. "Leave my husband alone. His heart is poorly, and you'll kill him if you keep this up."

"I want money," Howell said. "And I don't care how I get it."

"How much money?" Mrs. Cheney inquired. "How much would it take to buy our freedom?"

"One thousand dollars," Howell said, naming a sum so vast it must have seemed unimaginable.

"And were I to give you one thousand dollars, would you let us go?"

"Yes, I would."

This sum, in gold, it seems, had been buried in the yard at the commencement of hostilities, and, when Howell agreed to the terms set forth, Mrs. Cheney was sent to retrieve it in the company of one of Howell's men, a soft-faced, young lieutenant named James.

But when the two returned with the ransom, as promised, Howell told Cheney he was going to kill him anyway.

"But since you're a white man," he said, "I'll count to five so you can say your prayers."

"Hold on, Bub," said Howell's lieutenant, a young man who seems to have some faint trace of humanity left in his murdering bones. "Bub, you made a bargain, and you should stick to it."

"I don't make bargains with nigger lovers."

"But you made one just the same. You gave your word, and you ought to stick to it. Doing otherwise wouldn't be honorable."

But this appeal to "Southern Chivalry" went unheeded, and again Howell put his pistol to Mr. Cheney's head.

"When the day comes that I am captured," he told the doomed man, "it is I who will be killed and sent to hell, but for now it is you."

And with that, he pulled the trigger.

Now, Major John. B. Smithson with two hundred Illinois regulars and a force of militia is in pursuit. But the countryside in these parts is disloyal, and Howell will doubtless find succor there. It is in these rural places where men like Howell can play upon the longings of farm boys such as his naive, young lieutenant, and, from their ranks, gain the recruits they need. There shall be no peace in Missouri until these nest-holes of treason are cleaned out, one by one.

12
May 1865
Cobb P. Hill, Guest at Quantrill Reunion
Keatsville, Missouri

I never had no quit in me.

The night we voted quit we stayed in Billy Drury's barn. I wasn't for hiding out there because I never trusted him. Jess said Billy's people were good people, but Billy was not trustworthy in my eyes.

"You all make yourselves to home, now," Billy said.

He was a stubby man with a beard that most times had food stuck in it. He was good with horses, but he liked them better than he liked people, and I could never trust such a man as that.

He brought us supper—beans boiled in salt pork but no meat or bread. There was less than a dozen of us left in what had once been Bub Howell's command, but Billy still didn't have enough plates.

"You boys be leaving in the morning?" he asked, ladling out those damn beans.

I make no accusations. I only say that Billy Drury liked horses better than people, that he cut himself off from the world, and that betrayal was in the air.

When the Federals got Bub, they cut off his head and stuck it up on a telegraph pole. They dragged the rest of him behind a mule to Concord and set that up with a sign saying this was the fate of all guerrillas.

I didn't want them to do that to me. Still, I wasn't for quit.

"Beans, Jess?" Billy Drury said as he walked among us. "Coffee, Tom? Beans, Dick? We got plenty."

I make no accusations, but say again, betrayal was in the air.

Captain Sturgis had found us, earlier. He gave us a talk as we ate. Him and his men had quit two weeks before, and he said we should think about quitting, too. Bobby Lee had quit in Virginia, he said. He said there was nothing wrong with quitting when you were beat.

"The Federals will parole you. Just like regular soldiers, all you'll have to do is take the Loyalty Oath."

Tom Novinger said, "I swear no false oaths."

"I swore it," Dick said. "There's nothing wrong with swearing the Oath."

Dick Sturgis was a traitor—that's what I think. I think he quit and the Yankees spared him on the condition he go out and get others to quit. If Bub had been living, he would have killed Sturgis. He would have killed Billy Drury, too.

"I don't trust the Federals," Tom Novinger said. "They never once acted honorable in the whole war, and you're a fool if you believe they will now. And what is left for us to go home to? Our farms have been burnt. Our wives have been made impure."

"I got no quit in me," I said.

"It ain't about quit," Sturgis, the traitor said.

I started to say, "Is too," but I stumbled on the "t" and it came out stuttered, like a hundred rifle-guns going off one after the other—tat, tat, tat.

When I was a boy everyone laughed at me for this stutter. It was God's creation, but still they laughed. Then, one day, I laughed along with them, and it was less hard after that. When I laughed along, I was in on the joke and not just the butt of it. Still, I never talked much.

"It's quit," I said, "and quit is all."

"We ought to vote," Jess said. His courage had started to flag towards the end. He'd been a tiger at the start, but I hadn't seen the tiger in months. Sometimes, now, his hands would shake so hard that he couldn't load a revolver.

I told Jess, "Your brother got no quit in him." Frank had went with Quantrill to try and kill Lincoln. Booth only got there first.

Jess shook his head. "Ain't about quit."

"Is too," I said, and I didn't stutter.

Dick Sturgis said, "There's just no more sense to warring. Bobby Lee quit, and there's nothing wrong if you quit, too. Men are turning themselves in all over."

Tom Novinger was still a man. "Some things are more important than living," he said.

Jess's people try to tell you he wasn't for quit, but he was. Even they admit it was him who carried the white flag. If Jess wasn't for quit, then why did he carry the white flag? Ask his people that if you will.

The next day we started out towards the Arsenal at first light. As we left, I told Billy Drury I was on to him.

"Watch your step," I said.

He tried to laugh it off, but he was scared. He had neither principles nor honor. I should have gone back and killed him.

We rode right on down the highway like we owned it. When people saw us some waved and some ran. I liked that. Everybody knew Bub Howell's Boys.

When we got towards Arsenal Hill, twenty or so militia come up the road towards us. Jess waved that white flag, but the militia never respected such things.

Pop. Pop.

They started shooting.

Pop. Pop.

Tom Novinger went down.

There was but a dozen of us, but militia never were much, and when we charged, they broke like nothing. But about fifty regulars come up right behind them—Wisconsin boys—and once they got into it, there wasn't much left for Bub Howell's men.

The horses screamed. The men went down, but not Dick Sturgis. He was up in the van but untouched. He ran for it when it started. I make no accusations but only ask why.

My horse fell and me with it. Jess reached down and gave me a hand up behind him. I could see blood on his shirt, but he still got me up. He could be a man when he wanted. I give him that.

"Go," I said, once I was up.

He gave his horse the spur and we commenced to run, but four Wisconsin boys singled us out and charged. Jess got one, but the next got him, and the next one after got his horse.

I scrambled away, but the horse fell dead atop Jess, and he got pinned to the ground. The Federals fired at him. He fired back and struggled to pull free, but they hit him again. I figured that settled his accounts.

I ran, and the Wisconsin boys pursued me. I got shot in the heel but didn't fall. I started hobbling. I figured I was going to die, regardless, and I thought of Tom Novinger's words about there being things more important than life, so I wheeled and fired.

Pop.

I got one, and I laugh still when I think of the surprise on his face.

I got him from fifty yards with a pistol, and when he went down, it gave the others pause. They'd never seen shooting like that, and they wanted no part of me.

Now, that is ten thousand years gone by, and we hold reunions. We set up a picture of Quantrill, all framed up in a big, gilt frame. We set around it, and tell stories about the old days. When the dinner bell rings, we all let out a rebel yell and hobble over to the tables. But we're dying, one by one, and there aren't six of us fit enough to be pallbearers. It's a useless fate.

13

December 1865
Dr. Tyler Stemp, Physician and Pharmacist
Kearney, Missouri

I was thirty-two years old when the surrender came and, like a weary child, I just wanted to go home. I was a surgeon under Sterling Price and Sidney Marion Keats, and I had seen too much. So when Jax Brown called me into his tent—that last, mad night in camp—and informed me of his plan for empire, I was less than receptive.

"Are you still a patriot, sir? Do you still believe in honor?"

Hopes, dreams, bitterness, and fear all mingled in the air that night, rising, like vapors, to infect all who breathed them.

"Do you love the South, sir?" Jax Brown asked. "Do you believe in glory?"

"No," I shook my head. "Not any more. I believed in all those things, once, but I've seen too much death and too many horrors."

"But the horror is the beauty, and death is glory."

"No," I said, "I wish you good fortune, but no. I'm going home."

The next day, Brown led all that would follow to Mexico—the soldiers of the Lost Cause. They planned to offer their services to the Emperor Maximilian, but the rest of his plan was more a dash of the dice than a real possibility—the romantic hope that a new Southern empire would rise in Texas, perhaps.

Jason Alexander Xerxes Brown. He sensed, I think, that I was different from him and his fellows—perhaps in the same way that a wolf knows the members of his own pack from all others.

So Jax Brown and his cavaliers rode for the Rio Grande and glory, while I headed for Missouri and home. I knew, of course, that things had changed in Clay County, but in my heart I didn't imagine home would be much different than it had ever been. I imagined that I would pick up the threads of my life and carry on much as I had before—working with my father as a country doctor and pharmacist.

But Clay, and all of Western Missouri, was in a shambles. In some sections you could walk for miles and see nothing but burned out farms. Whole towns had been depopulated. Wandering veterans gathered in camps along the roadsides, slept in train stations, or lingered on street corners, picking quarrels with Negroes. Some of Quantrill's men went on raiding and robbing as if the war were still going full blast, fighting pitched battles with Home Guards and vigilance committees.

Frank and Jesse James were not among the latter, however. They, instead, returned to their mother's farm, intent on settling down. At the time, they were no more notorious than a thousand other men, and no one seemed to be out to get them, as their defenders sometimes claim.

Jesse, however, was not well. He had been wounded in the lungs towards the end of the war and was one of my father's medical patients. He had his ups and downs, but, from what I could see, he seemed well on his way to recovery. Then, one cold day, right around Christmas, Frank dashed into my father's pharmacy in an agitated state.

"Where's your father?" he demanded.

I told him that father was out on a case, and that I didn't expect him back until supper.

"Well, that beats it," Frank said.

He was twenty-three years old and slender, almost to the point of being gaunt. He wore an old overcoat he had stripped from the body of a Union soldier towards the end of the war, and underneath it, he wore guns.

"Jesse's worsened," he told me. "He's in great pain and we're nearly out of laudanum."

"That's strange," I said. I'd made him up a fresh bottle, not two days before.

"Strange or not, Jesse's in misery, and if we can't get your father, we'll have to make do with you."

Frank didn't trust me because I'd taken the infamous Loyalty Oath when I'd gotten home. If I hadn't, I might have been denied the right to practice my profession, but that didn't matter to a die-hard rebel like Frank.

"Are you coming?" he demanded.

"Of course I'm coming," I said. "But you're got to give me a moment."

I closed the pharmacy and wrapped myself in my coat and muffler. I went to the barn, out back, and hitched horse to buggy. Then, Frank and I made the best speed we could, considering we had to stop to cut fallen branches off the road every mile or so—axes and shovels were an important part of a doctor's medicine bag in those days.

"I hope we're not too late," Frank kept saying.

"I doubt that he's going to die," I told him.

The James house was, in reality, two houses. The newer place was set against the older one—so the two formed a T shape—and as the newer one was where the bedrooms were, Frank led me in.

We found Jesse flat on his back in bed, begging his mother for laudanum, despite the fact that she'd given him over two dozen drops throughout the morning.

"Oh, my poor baby," she exclaimed. "You've got to do something, doctor. You simply must."

Jesse's eyes were drowsy and the pupils were constricted from all the laudanum he had taken. I assured his mother that I'd make him feel better, then asked her and Frank to leave. I gave Jesse a spoonful of syrup and told him it contained laudanum, although it did not. Then I examined him as best as I could—there was a Colt's Navy revolver tucked under his pillow—and, as I suspected, I found no physical reasons for the degree of discomfort he seemed to be having.

"Feeling some relief now?" I asked, although the syrup I'd given him could have done nothing.

"Yes. It's some better. But the pain will come back. It always does, and it always will."

I'd seen symptoms similar to Jesse's in other soldiers who'd lived for months with terrible pain. Many became addicted to the morphine or laudanum that was used to fight the pain. Others, like Jesse, had been so worn down by agony that they lived in terrible fear of it.

"It has been eight months," I told Jesse. "Your wounds have healed, and I don't think you need so much laudanum anymore."

"How do you know what I need?" he said. He turned on his side to face the wall. "Everybody thinks they know what I need."

I asked him if he had a girl, and he said that he did, but that she lived in Kansas City.

"Would you like to see her?" I asked.

"Not while I'm like this," he said.

I patted him on the shoulder and told him to be brave—or some silly words to that effect—then went into the old part of the house to discuss the problem with Frank and his mother.

In one room, a kitchen and sleeping quarters for the servants, Loretta, the cook, made biscuits. In the other, a sitting room, a big, orange cat lay stretched out upon the hearth and two hound dogs scratched at their fleas.

Frank sat by them, reading. Dr. Reuben Samuel, the boy's stepfather, "Pappy" as Frank and Jesse called him, sat across from Frank, gazing into the fire. The boy's mother, sat next to him, in an old rocking chair, her hands busy at needlepoint.

"Dr. Samuel," I said. "How are you feeling these days?"

The Yanks had strung him up from a tree during the war and, since then, he'd had spells. I took his hand. It seemed firm and strong.

"Remembering things pretty well, are you?"

"Oh, yes, pretty well." He nodded his head then shrugged his shoulders.

Frank put down his book.

"Pappy's just fine," he said. "It's Jesse we've brought you for."

Tears were in Mrs. Samuel's eyes. "Oh doctor, why has the Lord singled out my poor boy for such misery?"

"Physically," I said, "Jesse is in the best condition he's been in for months. I don't believe that his pain is as great as he believes it to be, or that he needs his laudanum so much as he needs the idea of it. We must try our hardest to wean him off the drug."

"But I just can't bear to see that poor boy suffer," Mrs. Samuel said.

"I don't mean you should deny him his medication," I told her. "Only that Jesse must be made to recognize that his pain is not as great as is his fear of it. He tightens his muscles to fight the pain, and, in doing so, makes it all the worse."

I told them I had seen this kind of addiction before, and that I could cut the dosage without Jesse's knowledge, simply by reducing the amount of laudanum in the tincture when I mixed it.

Frank nodded his head. "It's a thing that should be done."

After more discussion, Jesse's mother went to comfort her son, taking Dr. Samuel with her, and I was left alone with Frank. He was something of a bookworm, dedicated to Shakespeare, Rousseau and the works of Robert Ingersoll, the famed agnostic. But the book he had in front of him, now, was something very different—Five Weeks in a Balloon, by Jules Verne—and, to make conversation, I asked how he was enjoying it.

"Why it's so light," he said, "it floats away."

That was Frank's idea of a joke. But the attempt had been there, and I hoped it meant a truce had been signed between us. He offered me a drink of whiskey, and, knowing this to be something of a rite of passage among my fellow rebels, I took him up on his offer

"Jesse told me he has a girl," I said. "But that he hasn't seen her in sometime."

"Yes, she lives in Kansas City."

"Well, get her here. Have her nurse him. She'll do more good than all of us."

"Yes," Frank ruminated, "I see your point. But Jesse's a high strung boy, and he's led the most thrilling of lives. He's walked the valley of the shadow of death. Farm life can't compare to what he's known."

"But farming is the life you're cut out for."

"The life we're cut out for is war."

Perhaps I was able to pick up the threads of my own life with more success than Frank and Jesse because I was a little older than they. I had adult memories connected to something other than war and slaughter, after all. I remembered warm beds and civilized evenings—wine and cigars and pleasant chats with ladies and gentlemen.

Or perhaps the animalcules that swam in their bloodstreams were somehow more primitive than those that swam in mine. When the chill winds howled down from the north my own, natural inclination was to seek home and shelter. But perhaps dimmer and more ancient memories caused men like Jax Brown and his wolves to draw their sabers and howl at the moon.

14
Spring 1866
Billy Drury
Farmer
Clay County, Missouri

I timed my entrance perfect at Jesse's baptism—missing the God part and the dunking business but arriving in time for the food.

"I'm so sorry, ma'm," I told his ma, as I stepped onto their back porch. "My riding horse come up lame, you see, and I had to foot it over to the landing and catch the stage..."

"That's all right, Billy," his ma said. A busy woman she was, that afternoon.

"You just help yourself. We got chicken and corn steamed in the husk. We got turnips and ribs. Biscuits and syrup. We got baked apples and cobbler."

She gave me a wink. "And I hear a flying rumor that Mr. Frank has a jug down behind the icehouse."

"Is that so?" I sniffed the air but detected nothing.

The place overflowed with people, all diehard rebels and ex-guerrillas—Cole Younger among them. Everyone was dressed in their Sunday best, and the bees were buzzing in the sweet pea vines that twined up along the porch.

Later on, after the boys became famous, the press referred to the place as "The Castle James," but on this day it was just a pleasant, old country farm—nothing more, nothing less. And it was planted, besides. Most men came back from the war to burnt out farms and had trouble coming up with the seed money needed to start afresh. But it was apparent that Frank and Jesse hadn't, for which I was glad.

I had no idea, at the time, that they'd been among the dozen or so ex-guerrillas who'd robbed the Jefferson Savings Association in Liberty—on St. Valentine's Day, no less. They'd shot down an innocent college student and fled with seventy thousand in currency, coin, and negotiables. Cole Younger, I later learned, had been among them.

"Cole," I said to him now. He was standing around in the yard, useless, holding a cup of punch and a pork chop.

"Billy," Cole said to me.

"How's old Sam Patch doing, these days?"

"Sam Patch?" Cole pondered, as if to pretend he didn't recall that beautiful thoroughbred he'd borrowed from me back at the start of the war.

After that little chat, I said hello to the boy's stepfather, Dr. Samuel that is, and he seemed chipper enough.

"Been doin' some plowin'," he told me.

"The place looks fine," I said.

Then I went on over to where the guest of honor stood—all spiffed up in his Sunday best and grinning from ear to ear, but a bit uncomfortable looking, I'd say. A line had queued up in front of him, and they came by, one by one.

"I'm so happy for you," they'd say. "You're looking so well. We're all very thankful."

"Yes. Yes," Jess would say. "There's cold punch up on the porch. We'll have pie later."

I pumped his hand when I got to him.

"Glad to see you looking so fit," I said.

"I still have some pains," he told me. "And I still cough from deep down but, with the Lord's help, I'll be back to singing in the choir one day."

"Well," I said, "whatever comes I'm glad to see you've made things right with your god, getting baptized and all."

He grinned and quoted some Bible do-dad or other. "'Except a man be born again, he cannot see the kingdom of God.'"

The young woman standing at his side corrected him.

"'Except a man be born of water...'"

Jess just laughed. "You know Miss Zerelda Mimms, don't you, Billy?"

"Well, no," I said. "I don't believe I've ever had the pleasure."

I couldn't help but grin. Nothing could have made me happier than to see a boy like Jess—who'd had so much bad luck in his life—standing next to a fine, upstanding Southern woman like Zee Mimms. Tall, slender, dark haired, and strong, she was—just the sort a young farmer might want to take for a bride.

"Mr. Drury." She offered her hand. "I've heard ever so much about you."

"Likewise, I'm sure."

Jess had had a crush on her since the war, when she'd nursed him.

"Jesse tells me that you offered shelter and comfort to our brave Rangers during the war," she said. "For that we will be eternally grateful, sir."

"Oh, weren't nothin'," I said. And it hadn't been, either. I had, indeed, given the guerrillas shelter, but I hadn't had much choice in the matter. What else can a man do but comply when a score of fellows with guns ride up to his door and ask to spend the night?

"Jess is a credit to the Southern cause," I said to Zee—a politic fellow, I was, and a politic woman, she was, too. She leaned over and whispered in my ear.

"A little bird tells me that Mr. Alexander Franklin James has a jug hid out somewhere down behind the icehouse."

Well, I always was a fellow who could take a hint, so I started down towards the icehouse, calling out Frank's name every now and again. When I found him, he was sitting propped up against the icehouse wall, his arms wrapped around the jug in question. Alongside him was none other than my old

75

friend and neighbor Sidney Marion Keats—General Keats, he was now, C.S.A., retired.

"Why, Billy. Billy Drury," Sid Keats said. "I haven't seen Billy Drury in a coon's age," he told Frank.

He'd put on a bit of weight since I'd last seen him, and the Yankees had burned his plantation and ropewalk to the ground. But, by in large, he seemed the same old Sid Keats he'd always been.

"You don't grow hemp, anymore, do you Billy?"

"No sir, haven't for some years. Just couldn't make it pay."

"I'm out of that business myself, now," he said. "Don't know what I'll do instead. Breed mules, maybe. But I've always been an optimist. The Lord, I've found, lights the way for His righteous children."

He took the jug from Frank. "We got liquor, Billy. Awful liquor it is, but liquor still. And beggars can't be choosers these days."

He pulled down his tie so as to avoid gagging, took a swig, then passed the jug back over to Frank.

"As my brother is saved by water," Frank said, "so I shall be saved by whiskey." Three sheets to windward, he was.

"Ignore the drunkard," Sid Keats laughed. "He saved my life during the recent unpleasantness, and I shall always be in his debt. But today, he is a drunkard, plain and simple. Incapable of serious thought."

I changed the subject. "Fine young woman Jess seems to have picked out," I said.

The two of them, Jess and Zee, were sitting together on the front stoop of the main house, now, and she was feeding him— you know, how lovers do. She'd pick a little, bitty bite of chicken off the bone and hold it up to his mouth.

"Have they set the date, yet?" I asked.

Frank shook his head. "Her family is opposed. My brother's an ex-bushwhacker and there are men who are out to get him."

"But the war's over," I said.

"The war will never be over," Sid Keats told me.

Frank shook his head and, as was his habit, let fly with a quotation himself. It ran in the family, I believe.

"'He that hath wife and children, hath given hostages to fortune; for they are impediments to great enterprises, either of virtue or mischief.'"

"You don't say," I said.

As it developed, the boys' next "great enterprise" took place over in Lexington—about thirty miles east of my little farm. Nobody knows who it was, exactly, but around noon one day, four men entered the bank, pointed their revolvers at the cashier, robbed him of two thousand dollars, and made their getaway without mishap.

A year later, in the spring of sixty-seven, six rough looking men sashayed into the bank in Savannah, Missouri, just north of St. Jo, killed the bank president but ended up with nothing for their troubles. Then, in May, a dozen ex-bushwhackers robbed the bank in Richmond, gunned down the mayor and two other men. The citizens didn't take kindly to these shenanigans, and the day after the robbery, they broke into the hoosegow, dragged out some unfortunate ex-guerrilla and strung him up on general principles.

In November, someone took a bank in Independence, just across the line from me—the Missouri River line, that is. Two men walked into the bank, robbed the vault, then locked the bank president and the teller inside.

Later that winter, Jess stayed at my place one night.

He rode in either very late or very early, depending on your point of view. When the dogs woke me with their barks, I thought, at first, it was wartime again, and guerrillas or militia were pounding on my door.

"Hello, Mr. Drury. Hello. Are you in there?"

"I should say I'm in here." I stumbled to the door and opened it. "But why in God's name are you here, now, Jess? It's well past midnight and freezing cold."

He stepped in and unwrapped the fur mufflers that covered his face. I hadn't seen him in a long time, but he was almost twenty-one years old by now and he'd filled out some. He looked more man then boy for the first time, in my opinion.

"Some men are after me," he said.

"Who?" I said.

"Militia come looking for revenge," Jess said. "One of 'em was one of those who strung up my stepfather. I shot the son of a bitch, but I think I only got him in the hip."

"That's terrible," I said.

He missed my meaning completely. "It was a hard shot," he said.

I invited him in and took a quick look out the door. The silver moon was lighting up the snow very brilliant, but I couldn't see anything unusual.

"I can't stay at home for a while," Jess said. "Do you mind if I stay here, just tonight?"

"Why, no, Jess. Stay all you want." I still didn't have any idea it was him and Frank who'd been robbing all those banks.

"Do you mind if I put my horse in your barn?"

"Why sure, sure. You go out and take care of your animal, then we'll have a chat if you'd like."

When Jess went out, I piled some more wood in the stove to warm things up and got some coffee brewing. When he came back, he went straight to the stove, shivering like he was cold all over. He just stood there, warming his hands and rubbing them together. His eyes darted this way and that—more nervous than I'd ever seen him.

"I just don't know," he said at last. "It's such an awful quandary. Goddamn, I've made a mess of things." He shook his head. "You don't know how big a mess."

"Want some coffee?" I said. "Need some food? How are you getting on with Miss Mimms?"

He opened the iron door of the stove.

"We can't get married when there are men out to kill me. And my damn lungs. In weather like this they always get worse. Damn."

He jammed a piece of stove wood into the flames. I did my best to comfort him.

"Things work out, you know. We worry and worry, but generally speaking, things do work out."

"Not for me," Jess said. He took another stick of wood and broke it in two. "Nothing ever seems to work out." He turned and faced me.

"You got any laudanum, Billy?"

15

Summer 1868
Warren Ashby, Bookstore Owner and Postmaster
St. George, California

Her ghost first appeared one morning as I washed the breakfast dishes. She stood in the tall pines beyond the creek that runs behind my little cottage. She wore that same spring frock—the color of daisies—that she'd worn on the day, so long ago, when I'd left home. Her hair was plaited in a long braid that dangled down and swung so gaily behind her. She came, barefooted, through the timber to the creek. She looked right and left, then sat herself down, and laughed as she played her hands in the cold, rushing water.

That happened on a Sunday, but it all began the Friday before, when a certain young man came into my store to post a letter. He was a good looking fellow who had gone native—in blue jeans, a flannel shirt, and a big, floppy hat. He was indistinguishable from the thousands of other seekers who came and went in the diggings in those days. I doubt I would remember him now—despite the fame he later gained—had he not stirred up Caroline's ghost.

"Can you tell me where the graveyards are?" he asked.

"The graveyards," I said.

"Yes. At the hotel they said you could tell me where the old graveyards were and where the first Baptist church used to stand. They said you were an old timer."

"I suppose I am."

He told me that his father had come west in 1850 to look for gold but had never come back, and I replied that there was nothing unusual in that.

"We all intended to return, but most of us didn't, for one reason or another."

"I'm searching for his grave," he said, "and I think it's somewhere nearby. The last letter he sent came from here, from when the town was called Gimcrack."

I nodded my head. "The name seemed indecent so we changed it."

"He was a reverend," the young man continued. "Since you were here back then, I wonder if you might remember him? The Reverend Robert James?"

I thought for what seemed a respectful moment.

"The name calls up no particular recollection. We had so many itinerant preachers in those days. It's difficult to say. I'm sorry."

"Well," he said, "I hadn't expected much. Perhaps you can take care of this for me."

He handed me the letter he wanted posted, and when I saw it was addressed in care of the postmaster in Kearney, Missouri—my own home state—my attitude towards him took a sudden change. I put on my homiest grin.

"You know, cousin," I said. "I'm from Howard County myself. Near Fayette."

He hesitated, as if something in this bothered him, then said he knew it well and offered his hand.

"J. W. James," he said, "from Clay. Pleased to meet you."

He inquired again about the Baptist church, and I told him no churches had even existed around here until a couple of years after the goldrush.

"So if your father died in fifty, I don't think looking in church graveyards would do much good. His grave probably isn't even in town. It's more likely to be up any of a score of creeks and canyons. And if it was ever marked, it probably isn't anymore. Honestly, cousin, I'd say you could search for all eternity and never find what you're looking for."

"Regardless," James said, "I intend to try."

He told me that he had come to San Francisco by way of Panama—then up the Sacramento by riverboat, to Placerville by rail, and St. George by stage. The journey had been uneventful, and his only complaint was that the fleas had been troublesome.

"But this mountain air is doing wonders for my lungs. And I can't get over all the Chinamen. I never even seen a Chinamen back home, and here they're all over... just scurrying along, pigtails and all."

I told him we had our own little Chinatown in St. George and he expressed a desire to visit it.

"I'm lodged at the Orleans Hotel," he said. "The food's good there, but they tell me Raffeto's Oyster House shouldn't be missed. If you'd care to join me there this evening, I'd be pleased to buy a fellow Missourian his supper."

I accepted his invitation and, when evening fell, met him at Raffeto's.

The restaurant stood in a rather substantial old house—with a stone foundation and even a basement—at the far end of Main Street. In more flush times, it had been the private dwelling of the owner of one of the tunnel companies, but when the tunnel went bust, Louie Raffeto bought it on the cheap and turned it into a restaurant.

Now, Louie and his family lived upstairs. The bar and kitchen occupied the first floor. The dining room inhabited the basement. The tables were draped with checkered table cloths, and, as the Raffetos were great lovers of cats, a dozen or more of the little animals, always roamed free on the floor, begging food and jumping, uninvited, into the laps of the patrons.

After we had been seated, James asked me what was recommended on the bill of fare. As oysters and clams—freighted up daily from San Francisco Bay—were the specialty of the house, I suggested we start off with an appetizer of oysters and bacon on buttered toast.

James enjoyed these very much and seemed unconcerned about the high prices. He struck me as either a free spender or as someone who was trying to impress his guest.

We drank plenty of red wine and followed the oysters with a steaming tureen of Mrs. Raffeto's minestrone soup, which, along with lots of hot bread, formed the main course. We finished off the meal with a dessert that was a blend of soft ice cream and rum, and by that time, James was talking with abandon.

"I was pretty small when he left," he said of his father. "I'm not even sure if I remember it, if I just dreamed it, or if somebody told it to me. I can hardly even picture him."

I waited for more but no more was forthcoming. James merely laughed and shook his head, as if in fond remembrance, then, without warning, grew angry.

"He shouldn't have abandoned us."

Apprehending at once, Mr. James' mercurial nature, I tried to sooth him by saying again that we had all come to the diggings—even the Chinese—with the intention of making a big strike then returning to our homes.

"I left my own sweetheart behind when I came," I told him.

"Then you abandoned her, too."

"I intended to go back but..." I fished for a euphemism. "But something important happened."

"What could be more important than your sweetheart?"

We fell silent after that, but just as the quiet was becoming oppressive, a mewing kitten came round to our table. James laughed and picked the tiny thing up in his big hand.

"I don't even know what I'll do if I find his grave," he mused. "Just stand there and look at it, I guess."

We drank more red wine after that—lifting several toasts to our home state— then we ordered more oysters—mostly for the cats—and by the time I returned home, I must admit, I wasn't walking a very straight line. I recall whistling some happy tune to myself as I entered my little cottage and fell into bed.

I slept in fits and woke a number of times in the night, dreaming hot, troubled dreams—I was back home, in Missouri, and I'd returned to look for my sweetheart. But in the dream, I couldn't find her. I wandered town and country, looking and coming close, but never quite finding. It was a dream I'd dreamed a thousand times before but not in many years.

On the night before I'd left Missouri—in the spring of 1849—Caroline had expressed worry over the possibility that I might not return. The trip was dangerous. The Far West was wild and lawless.

I remember how she looked up at me, as we embraced— the tears in her eyes. She pressed her beautiful face against my chest.

"Oh," she said, in mock anger. "If you don't come back I'll be so mad at you."

That winter, while I was in California, she came down with a quartan fever and the shivers and sweats. They bled her four times a day for five days and, on the last day, begging to be bled again, my darling Caroline died.

In the morning, I awoke from my dream teary eyed and fretful. I cooked my breakfast and ate with care, then stood at the kitchen window, cleaning the dishes. Outside, the world was alive with hammering woodpeckers and scurrying lizards. The trees were filled with squirrels. It was a beautiful, summer morning, but it seemed oppressive to me. I put on my coat and went to the store.

Late that afternoon, James came in to post another letter. He'd searched all the graveyards, he said, but hadn't found anything.

"I'm sorry to hear that," I told him.

"I won't rest until I find it."

The letter he gave me was addressed to his brother in Paso Robles, California. From what he said, I gathered that this brother had accompanied him on the journey west, but had lingered at their uncle's place, down south, rather than searching for their father's grave, and James was rather miffed about it.

"But this morning," he said, brightening, "someone told me of a place called Missouri Canyon."

"Yes," I said. "It's north of here, towards the Middle Fork. A number of Missourian's lived there once. It might be a good place to try."

"I intend to head out for there tomorrow," James said.

"But don't get your hopes too high," I cautioned.

"Yes. I understand... I could wander forever and never find him."

We shook hands. I thanked him again for the dinner at Raffeto's and he bid me goodbye.

That was the last I ever saw of J. W. James, but that night I dreamed of Caroline again.

Again, I wandered the graveyards of Howard County— seeking but never finding. Again, I awoke with tears in my eyes. Again, I rose and made my coffee and fried my bacon. I stood at the window, cleaning the dishes.

And there she was, wrapped in the lush, green of the world, coming down through the timber, dressed all in white and barefooted, with daisies in her hair—all youth and beauty and things gone by. She stood by the creek and looked about. She sat down. She put a foot in the water, then pulled it out, as if the water were too cold.

I went down the backstairs and crossed the creek on the backs of the smooth, round stones that stretched across it. I called to her, but she did not hear. When I reached the other side, I squatted down beside her and spoke. Still, she didn't hear. I touched her shoulder but felt nothing.

Now, she eased her foot into the water, and I realized that the creek seemed swollen. The water rushed past us, and the stones I'd walked across were nowhere to be seen. It was as if here, on this ghostly side of the creek, it was spring and the snows were melting. But on the other side, in the world of men and shattered dreams, it was summer, and the waters were shallow and still.

"Caroline," I said.

She looked up and glanced back, over her shoulder, as if she had heard, then she turned away again.

I sat with her on the bank, by the gay, rushing water, for the longest time. I talked to her. I told her how unhappy I was without her. I told her I never should have left. Then, without saying a word, she stood, looked down at where I sat, then turned and walked back towards the timber.

"Goodbye," I called, but she didn't answer.

I wondered, for a long time after that, if seeing Caroline's ghost would somehow heal my wounds, but ghosts such as her, who haunt—not graveyards and attics, but hearts and dreams—can never be exorcised. Even now, when I sleep, I often journey back to green Missouri and the graveyards of Howard County. I search and search but never find. In the morning, I awake, teary eyed and weeping. I make my breakfast and watch for her. I clean the dishes.

On certain mornings, when I feel I cannot bear it any longer, I write her letters in slow and flawless script. When they're done and perfect, I crumble up each page, put it in a teacup and light it with a candle flame. The smoke curls upwards, and when it disappears, I put on my coat and go to work. What else can one do?

16

December 1869

THE ST. LOUIS UNION

BANK ROBBERY AND MURDER

—✶—

A Useless and Wanton Slaying
A Bold and Daring Escape
The Outlaws Identified

The same robber gang that has been blamed for countless robberies in this state struck the bank at Gallatin yesterday. Usually, a dozen or more of these ex-bushwhackers are needed to carry out such depredations, but at Gallatin only two bandits were required to kill one man, wound another, and relieve The Grand River Savings Association of some $800.

Both were dressed in long, soldier's overcoats. They entered the town at about two o'clock and dismounted. While one held their horses, the other entered the bank alone. Described as youthful and steely-eyed, he presented the cashier, Captain Harrison W. Deering, with a $100 bill and asked for change. But as Captain Deering complied with this mundane request, a look of recognition came over the young man's face.

"You're the son of a bitch who murdered Bub Howell," he said.

The bandit drew his revolver and fired twice, hitting Captain Deering square in the heart and, as he fell, the head.

At that, the second bandit, tall and slender, rushed into the bank.

"What in the devil is going on in here?"

"Murder! Murder!" William P. Bluestone, the clerk, shouted.

"We won't have any of that, young man," the second bandit cautioned.

But when Bluestone persisted in his shouts, the second bandit opened fire, wounding Bluestone in the arm and shoulder.

The robbers then stuffed the contents of the cash drawer into a flour sack and rushed into the streets. But there, the citizenry, alerted by the sound of the gunshots, had gathered and armed themselves. When the robbers attempted to mount their horses, the men of the town opened fire.

The horse of the youthful bandit bolted at the sound, and the young man was dragged several feet before he could disentangle his foot from the stirrup. The tall one, who was by now some twenty yards away, wheeled his horse back into the teeth of the firing, rode to his fallen comrade and, with an air of calm, offered him a hand up.

"It was the most courageous act I ever saw," said John McFall, a lawyer of the town and a veteran of Chickamaugua and other campaigns.

The two bandits then made off, mounted double, but the mare they left behind, a thoroughbred, was recognized as belonging to a Clay County man named Jesse James. He and his brother rode under the notorious Arthur 'Bub' Howell during the war, and it is supposed that Captain Deering, the murdered cashier, was mistaken for the man who brought about Howell's death in 1864.

The capture of the bandits is thought imminent, and the people of the town are so incensed, that no one thinks justice will require a judge and jury.

OUTLAWS

George Jansen

17

July 1873
Michael T. Donlin, Baggage Master
Chicago, Rock Island & Pacific Railroad

In Ireland, the landlords tried to starve us, and in forty-seven—as if the starvin' weren't sufficient—they went and evicted us.

Me uncle Jerry had gone to America in the thirties—Boston, Massachusetts. He wrote home once a month, and his letters were full of money and wondrous tales—in America, you ate meat everyday, leastways accordin' to Uncle Jerry.

When I was fifteen years old, and I'd had enough of starvin', I told my dear mother I wouldn't stand for it no more. I was going through "The Golden Door" to America, I told her. I thought she'd raise a howl, but, instead, she asked me to take me little brother along.

"He'll die, sure, if he stays here."

Brendan was seven years old, was all, and he didn't want to go. Didn't want to leave his dear mother, but, God bless her, she lied to him in such a way as to convince him she was coming, too. She walked all the way to Cork with us—from County Waterford—just so he'd believe it. Half starved, herself, she was, and broken hearted, though she never let on.

As we was gettin' aboard the packet for Liverpool, mother told Brendan she had to attend to our luggage—of which we had none, of course—and we never saw her again. A beautiful woman she was—buck toothed and freckle faced, the map of Ireland writ large upon her, as the saying goes.

Brendan cried the whole way over. So did I—two months aboard the sailing ship West Wind, tackin' this way and tackin' that, livin' on deck, cookin' there, too, and, if that weren't enough, seasick most of the time. Hell's bells, anyone would've cried.

Once in America, Uncle Jerry got me into railroadin' as a day laborer. All you needed was a strong back in those days, and they were laying track so fast, the bosses had even stooped to employing Irishmen. Me and Brendan helped build the Erie and, after that, the Michigan Central.

For years we lived hand to mouth and day to day, but, still, it was better than starvin'. When the Civil War started, Brendan volunteered to go off and fight—the Twenty-third Illinois, the "Irish Brigade," it was called. He loved this here country, believed in it with all his heart—God bless him. So he went and died for his convictions, the damn silly bastard, and after all the trouble our dear mother had gone to.

Me, I wasn't so patriotic, and when Brendan and all the boys marched off, it so happened that native born labor run short, and I got hired on in a more substantial position—a brakeman on the Illinois Central.

No Christmas dinner, that, I learned—running across the top of the cars while the train was moving. Snow, wind, rain—it didn't matter to the railroad. The engineer would whistle "down brakes" and out and up I'd go.

I had two of me fingers crushed in the couplers in sixty-three. Almost lost a leg when I got pinned between cars in sixty-five. Then, a year later, the bleedin' company fired me for flattenin' too many wheels. That's capitalist gratitude for you.

I got a job as a baggage handler on the Rock Island road after that, which all brings me—at last, you say—to the time Jesse James wrecked and robbed us.

I was a regular on the Council Bluffs to Chicago run by then—a baggage master, no less. Our consist was about as usual that night—a baggage car, a combine, two Pullman sleepers, a half dozen day coaches, and a smoker. We took on the mail and a couple of passengers at Atlantic, and, after I stowed the baggage, I set down to stretch out me game leg.

So I'm dozin' there, quite peaceful and content, while Bill Royce, the messenger—all industry, Bill was, and a great lad—smokes a cigarette and does the mail registry.

Then the wheels screech—iron on iron. The whole train shakes and lurches, and I'm thrown forward onto the floor.

"What the devil?" I says to Bill.

Bill, who's on his hands and knees, groggy and rubbin' his head, says not a word. So I get to me feet, slide open the side door of the combine, and scramble down onto the embankment.

I have a look about and see that the locomotive is in the ditch, turned on her side, hissin' and spittin' like the great iron teakettle she is. The tender is still behind her, but twisted and half turned over. The baggage car is danglin' over the embankment. The combine's front trucks are derailed, but, behind that, the rest of the train looks all well and good.

Contemporaneous with this, I sees Heinie Roush, the fireman, climb out the wrecked cab up ahead, like a dead man rising. He starts up the embankment, stumbles towards me like a drunkard, and I calls to him.

"What the devil, Heinie?"

Heinie was contract labor—a Dutchman the bosses had brought over to work for scab wages—but I never held that against him. The bosses do as the bosses do, and the rest of us just tries to survive.

Well, Heinie's all black with soot, as always, but I can see, too, that he's got blood rushin' down his forehead like Niagara, which he's trying to staunch with an oily rag.

"I donts know whvat happen," says he. "I donts know whvat, but Hog is killed, I tink."

"Hog?" I says. Hog Kelly was the engineer that night. "Not Hog," I shakes me head. "It'd take more than a little wreck like this to kill that old hogger."

"Still, he's killed, I tink," says Heinie.

He tells me they were thunderin' down the track, full steam, when they saw that a rail was missing up the line—tore up by the Jameses it turned out. Hog threw her into reverse and slammed on the air-brakes, but too late.

"I never heard no whistle," I says.

"I don't tink ve did vhistle," says Heinie.

I tell him we ought to go see about Hog, but just then masked men start pourin' out of the bushes—a dozen or more—all along the length of the bleedin' train.

"Dey's shootin' at us," Heinie says.

"No," I say. "Why would they be..."

But then, I see the muzzle flashes and hear the pop, pop, pop. Some white-livered S.O.B. blows off a shotgun, and the shot splatters up against the side of the combine. I start to scramble back inside. I turns to give Heinie a hand up, but the little Dutchman just shakes his head.

"De boiler, she'll blow," he says, and he starts to run back towards the locomotive—through a hail of lead, as the saying goes.

So I climb up into the combine, and there's Bill Royce, the messenger, sittin' on the floor, calm and collected, rollin' himself a smoke.

"What the devil, Mick?" he says.

"Heinie says they've killed Hog."

"Whose killed Hog?" says Bill. "Calm down, Mick. We been in wrecks before."

"Not like this one," I tells him. I starts to point towards the open side door, and just as I do, a man wearing a flour sack over his head, with little holes cut for his eyes and mouth, climbs in. He points his big, black pistol right at me.

"Where's the money, you son of a bitch?"

This fellow, I later learned, was Jesse James, himself. Famous, he already was for robbin' banks, stagecoaches, and the Fairgrounds in Kansas City. More famous, still, he was about to become, for being the first man, ever, to wreck and rob a speeding, transcontinental express.

"Give up the keys or I'll kill you where you stand," Jesse says.

Another fellow—Cole Younger, it turned out—jumps into the combine right behind him. A big man, this one is, with hands like hams, whose face, like Jesse's, is hid under a flour sack.

"If he won't give up the keys," says Cole, "shoot the son of a bitch."

Jesse shoves his pistol into me ribs. "You heard him. Where are the keys?"

Coward that I am, I point at poor Bill Royce, froze to the floor with that damn cigarette, half-rolled and falling apart, dangling from his lips.

"That fellow there's got the keys, not me," I says, and Jesse turns towards Bill.

"Give up the keys or you're a dead man."

For a moment, Bill just sets there, and I fear he's gotten a notion into his head to do something foolish. But as it develops Bill's no more anxious to defend the honor of the bleedin' capitalists who own the bleedin' Rock Island than I am and, at last, he reaches around his belt to where his key ring is and takes it and skids it across the floor towards Jesse's feet.

"Get 'em!" Jesse says, and Cole snatches up the keys.

In a flash, he's got the safe open, and he's pulled out a leather pouch with a good two thousand dollars in it. But this ain't enough, it seems, for Mr. Jesse James.

"Where's the rest?" he says to Bill.

Bill shrugs his shoulders. "That's all there is."

"Like hell that's all," Jesse says. He goes over to Bill, picks him up by the shirt, stands him on his feet, and shoves the barrel of his pistol into Bill's nose—and I mean right up into it.

"Where's the goddamn bullion?"

"What bullion?" says Bill, the sweat pouring down his temples.

"The gold being shipped from Denver."

"I don't know about any gold."

"If you're lying I'll kill you," Jesse says.

"If the son of bitch won't tell, shoot him!" Cole screams.

"I don't know anything about any gold. I swear to God I don't."

"Move over!" Cole shouts to Jesse. "Move over, and I'll kill him right now."

Jesse jumps out of the way. Cole sticks his gun in Bill's ear, cocks it, and pulls the trigger. The gun goes "click," but, still, poor Bill faints dead away on the floor.

"Christ," Jesse says to Cole. "Why the hell did you go and do that?"

"You told me to," says Cole.

Now, Jesse pulls off his mask—the flour sack coverin' his head—and throws it on the floor of the combine.

"Where's the water bucket?" he says to me, and I points to it.

He goes and takes himself a drink from the dipper, then picks up the bucket and tosses what's left on poor Bill, who comes up, sputterin' and spittin'.

"Where's the gold from Denver?" Jesse says.

"I don't know anything about any gold," says Bill. "Believe me. I don't."

Meanwhile, Cole's been going through the car like a tornado—opening drawers, pulling bags off shelves, dumping their contents on the floor.

"I think he's tellin' the truth," he says to Jesse. "I don't think there's nothin' here."

Jesse turns to Cole, his face livid—red as beet. "You're the one who scouted this out. You're the one responsible. How come there's no gold?"

"Don't blame me. You're supposed to be the brains in this organization. That's what the newspapers tell me."

The two of them just stand there, starin' each other down and, for a minute, I think they're about to come to blows, themselves. But then, Jesse starts yelling at poor Bill again.

"How come there's no gold?"

Well, I'm gettin' pretty tired of the whole affair by this time, and I'm startin' to feel sorry for Bill—dripping wet and trembling from head to toe, he is.

"Look," I says to Jesse James, "I don't know anything about any gold, and I don't think this lad does either. But if you'll be nice and stop waving that pistol around, I might be able to take you to someone who does."

"And who would that be?" Jesse says.

"Tom Gable, the conductor. Usually he rides in the smoker."

"All right pard. You take me to this conductor of yours, but if you've lied, you know what's in store."

"I know," says I.

Well, the combine has both front and rear platforms and end doors, so I lead Jesse out the back end, whilst Cole stays behind and hunts for the supposed gold from Denver.

In the first coach, men, women, and children cower behind their seats and, in the second, the scene is much the same. In the third coach, two men are robbin' the passengers of their valuables, and some bleedin' Bible beater in a pigeon-tail coat is standin' up on one of the seats, hunched over 'cause of the roof, and shouting out prayers to God.

"Repent your sins before you die," he cries to the passengers, and then he tries to get them to sing.

"'We are climbing Jacob's ladder...'"

Pop! Pop! One of the robbers fires a pistol in his general direction.

"Keep down, you son of a bitch."

We enter the next coach—the fourth—and, just as we do, the door at the other end opens with a bang and here comes the conductor—Big Tom Gable, brass buttons and all—striding down the aisle towards us with a gun as big as Jesse's in his hand.

Jesse starts to yell at him, but before he can get the words out of his mouth, Big Tom's gun goes off, the passengers all scream, and Tom goes down in a heap on the floor.

"Oh, Christ," he screams. "Christ. Jesus. I been killed."

He starts runnin' his hands all over himself to try and figure where he's hit, but there ain't no blood. When Jesse gets to him, he kneels down and sticks his Colt's Navy in Tom's nose just like he did to poor Bill Royce.

"Where's the damn gold, you son of a bitch?"

"You've gone and killed me," Tom exclaims. "You done gone and shot me dead."

"No I ain't, you stupid fool. You tripped, is all, and your gun went off."

"You mean I ain't been shot?"

"No, you ain't, but if you want it to stay that way, you'd better tell me where the gold shipment is."

"Gold shipment? What gold shipment?" And Tom thinks for a minute. "Why, you've got the wrong train, sir. The gold's coming in on the next one, not this one."

We never did let him live that one down, trippin' over your own feet and thinkin' your shot is one thing, but callin' a train robber "sir" is another.

About this time, one of the fellows who'd been robbing the passengers in the third coach—Frank James, I later learned—steps into the car where we was.

"What the hell is going on?"

Jesse looks up at him. "There's no gold."

"What?"

"Cole got it wrong. The gold's on the next train, not this one."

"Ah, well," says Frank, undisturbed. "I got a good watch off some carpetbagger. What happened to your mask?"

"It got too hot," says Jesse, "so I took it off."

"Ought not go around without a mask," says Frank shaking his head.

"I can't breathe in it."

"Well, then, come help us rob the passengers."

"No." Jesse shakes his head. "We been here too long, already. We ought to be going."

"All right," says Frank. "Let's go, then."

He turns towards the passengers, raises his gun, fires it off, and everyone, including me, screams and ducks for cover. A minute later, when we're all brave enough to come up for air, it seems Tom Gable has got it in his head to go after Jesse again.

"Where's my gun?" says he, searchin' around on the floor.

"Don't you think you've pushed your luck enough for one night?" I says. "They killed Hog, you know."

"Hog?" says Tom. "Why would they kill Hog?"

"Well, I don't know, but Heinie says they did."

So the two of us climbs out of the coach and heads up towards the engine. And, sure enough, there's Hog lying dead on the embankment, with Heinie Roush beside him—a grown man, cryin' his eyes out.

"He never tooks his hand off deh trottle," says Heinie. "His neck broke, but he never let go deh trottle."

Hog became something of a hero that night, and the newspapers all told the story of the brave engineer. Fat lot of good it did his widow and children.

Heinie was a hero, too. Before he dragged Hog's body out of the locomotive, he put out the furnace fire and drained the water from the boiler. The whole thing might have blowed, killing a lot of innocents, if it weren't for that little Dutchman. He went back to Germany after his contract was up, but I don't know what happened to him after that.

Me, I never was a hero, not even for a minute. Just a working man is all.

In Ireland, the landlords tried to starve me. In America, me brother got blown to bits by a shell, and I got me two fingers crushed in the couplers between railroad cars. I got robbed by Jesse James in seventy-two. In seventy-seven I got me head broke open by a Pinkerton club when I struck for the union shop, and in eighty-six, I got beat up by the coppers in Chicago for singing "The Internationale"—"Arise ye workers from your slumbers. Arise ye prisoners of want."

So much for freedom of speech.

I saw a speaker in the union hall once, a fellow with little pince-nez spectacles and pasty, white hands—never worked a day in his life, I'll wager. But a learned fellow, he was, and, accordin' to him, great men are a product of their times and not the other way around. It's the dialectic, you see, manifesting itself through class struggle, that makes men what they are, leastways accordin' to this balmy bastard.

Me dear, departed mother might have called it, the inscrutable ways of the Lord—a braver woman never lived.

18

Summer 1873
Mrs. Frankie Dixon, Sharecropper and Cook
Keatsville, Missouri

My son, Buster, was a good boy—raw-boned and frolicsome. But when he was sixteen, he fell in with trash.

One day this white boy named Joe Sawyer, said to Buster, "I can go sell your horse over to Keatsville for good money, and we'll both make profits."

Buster said, "All right, you do that," and that was the start of his tribulations.

Buster was ignorant, that was his only failing. The horse was owned by him, sure thing, but he'd borrowed the money for it from Mr. Price Jackson, the white man who owns Jackson Farms down by Shoal Creek. Buster should've obtained Mr. Jackson's permission to sell that horse, but he didn't know. So, when the white boy sell it, Mr. Jackson put up a big disturbance, and the sheriff comes and arrests Buster and throws him into jail.

"The money don't matter," the sheriff said, when Buster offered to pay. "This is about principle."

My husband was croppin' for General Keats, then—we get half, the general get half, you know. I be a scull'ry maid, too, in the kitchen, so when I hear Buster got jailed I went straight to the general.

The general said, "Don't you worry about it, Miss Frankie. I'll go see the sheriff for you."

So the general went into Keatsville and paid Buster's bail—at least that's what he said he did.

But the general said to Buster, "You're paroled to me, now. I saved you, so you've got to work for me 'til you're all paid off."

No trial, no nothing. We s'posed to be free, but the general, he bought Buster just like he was a slave.

Listen. Back in the slavery-time, when the freedom come, we were all joyful.

"No more lickins'," we said, but they licked us still and kept us ignorant.

Listen. When the freedom come my mistress said, "Frankie, you ain't really free, you know. You got to stay here just like always, and you'll be better off, too."

In the slavery-time, I was owned by her husband—Mr. Otis, his name was, over in Ray County. When I was goin' on fourteen, Mr. Otis took a likin' to me.

I said, "Please don't, sir. I got my virtue."

But he don't take no for an answer. He gave me things—an old dress and some candy, once. When that didn't work, he said he's gonna lick me. When that didn't work, he held a razor to my throat. I lived with that, day after day, week after week, months and months and months.

When the baby came out, and it be plain the baby was half-white, Missy Otis she got all puffed up. She went ragin' through the house so bad, I feared she'd sell me south. Instead, she kept me around so as she could lord it over Mr. Otis.

Then, she made the driver lick me. My skin was flayed off my back, and the driver said, "I don't think she can stand no more, Missy."

Missy Otis said, "If you don't whip her, I'll have you whipped."

Then, when the freedom come, Missy, she got the nerve to tell me, "You know, Frankie, freedom doesn't really mean you're free. You're free to stay here is all it means. You're incapable of takin' care of yourself, you know."

101

Hubert Dixon, my husband, he be a shade or two darker than me. Buster—Mr. Otis his daddy—he be a shade or two lighter. One day, maybe there won't be no more shades at all. We'll all be just the same. Maybe then we all be free.

When we come to Keatsville and started 'croppin, Jesse James was a big, bad outlaw -- robbin' trains and banks all over, killin' sheriffs. None of the coloreds was s'posed to know who he really was, we was s'posed to think his name was Howard, but we all knew he was Jesse James.

Had a bad cough, I recollect—a ghostly man, he was.

The day the posse come for Buster—after he sold Mr. Jackson's horse—Jesse James was stayin' at the general's. When the posse came ridin' up, Jesse lighted out for the cookhouse where I happened to be workin'.

He run in, pull a gun, bolt the door, hide.

"Keep quiet, nigger," he said.

The posse didn't pay Jesse James no mind. No sir. They were after bigger game—Buster Otis.

Buster ran right to the general's house when he see'd the posse. He thought the general would protect him, but the general was in St. Louis buyin' artwork.

"Oh Lord, my Lord," I said, when I saw 'em grab him.

Jesse say again, "Be quiet, nigger."

They pulled Buster out the house, took him to jail, and gave him a lickin'. When the general bailed him out, Buster's face was all swelled up. He had four teeth knocked out, and his privates was all broke up.

I had to feed him like a baby, but three days later, the general came and put him to work.

I said, "Buster can't possibly work yet."

The general said, "I got to get my investment back."

He treated his horses better'n he treated Buster. Treated his dogs better.

When Buster been workin' months and months for the general, I went to see the general about it one day.

I said, "General, how long my boy gon' be workin' in the stables? My Hubert need him to help with the hemp."

The general showed me this paper. He said it was the terms of Buster's parole. He didn't know I could read, cause I always kept it secret. The paper was nothin' about parole. It was somethin' else again—a bill of sale for mules.

The general said, "I'm sorry, Miss Frankie, but, as you can see, my hands are tied."

The son of a bitch. But what could I do? What could I say?

One time, Jesse James and the general were out on the front grass. There was green lawn all around the house out there—real nice. The colored folks kept it trimmed. Them two—Jesse and the general—they were playin' croquet with Missy Keats and two more white women. I was in the kitchen yard washin' dishes, choppin' stove wood.

Jesse James, he hit the ball, and it goes in the wicket.

The general say, "Oh, good shot there, Mr. Howard."

The white womens all giggle. Jesse, he was partial to one of 'em.

She said, "Why, Mr. Howard, you are so manly."

Jesse James, all skinny and sunk-eyed, grinned at that—ghostly man, he was.

Two white men came ridin' up the lane just about then. General Keats walked out to meet 'em, but Jesse stayed back with the ladies.

General Keats started jawin'. "What can I do for you boys?"

The big one said, "My name's P. P. Ferris, and we come up from Kansas City, representin' the railroad and lookin' to buy some mules."

General Keats, he was breedin' mules, then, but he said somethin' else.

"I'm not sellin' any mules right now. You go down to Jackson Farms by Shoal Creek, if you want to buy some mules."

The big one, he had a monkey-face—little, tiny eyes, big old forehead.

"But Mr. Jackson sent us up here," he said. "Mr. Jackson said you were lookin' to sell."

Monkey man's friend, he was young and nervous. Both of 'em was wearing two pistols. The nervous one, he had a scatter-gun, too.

The general said, "My mules can't be beat, but I ain't sellin' right now. You go down to Jackson Farms, like I told you."

The monkey man tipped his hat, "I'll do that, sir." And they rode off.

Jesse James walked up to where the general was. They were still holdin' their croquet mallets. I was still washin' dishes.

The general said, "I ain't never seen any mule buyers go so heavily armed before."

Jesse James said, "Pinkertons."

That afternoon, he left.

The next time the posse came 'round, they were after the white boy, Joe Sawyer. He'd started stealin' horses outright 'bout then. The posse came, but they couldn't find Joe, so they fixed on Buster.

They caught him right on the general's front porch. He fought and kicked. Buster was big, but the posse was many. The sheriff took a hickory slat and brained him.

This time, the general was in his office, over by the side of the house, and when he heard the commotion he come runnin'.

"What the hell you doin' with my nigger?"

"He's been stealin' horses," the sheriff said.

General Keats had a big pistol in his hand, and he fired it off into the ground.

"You take your hands off that boy. If anyone lynches that boy, it'll be me."

The sheriff, he backed down and tipped his hat.

"Yes sir, general, sir."

I was glad the general saved Buster that time, but he was jus' doin' it 'cause Buster was his property. Dead nigger ain't worth nothin'—that's the way I estimates it.

One day that winter, Buster went into Keatsville with a load of firewood to sell, and the sheriff ain't got nothin' better to do than to come over and trouble him.

The sheriff said, "Those your mules, boy?"

"No, sir. Ain't my mules. Those are General Keats' mules."

"You stole those mules, didn't you? Just like you stole Mr. Price Jackson's horse?"

"No sir, I didn't steal no horse. I didn't steal no mules. Those are the general's mules, you know that."

"Some nigger 'round here been stealin' horses. You got anythin' to do with that?"

"No, sir. I'm a Christian man."

"You a nigger and you been stealin' horses. You and that white boy."

"No, sir. No-way. I never steal no horses. I sellin' firewood, is all. Please, sir, why do you do this to me all the time?"

"Just your bad luck," the sheriff said.

After that, Buster was mad as hell. He came home and said he was leavin'. He got an old pistol—the general's cap and ball gun—and he shoved it in his belt.

I said, "Buster, they'll set the nigger dogs on you if you run off with the general's pistol. Maybe all this'll pass, one day."

"I don't care," Buster said. "And this don't pass. Never."

Chicago, he say he goin' to. He say he going to write, too, but I never heard from him.

Terrorize. Lynch. White folks is a puzzlement.

19
November 1873
Colonel Jax Brown, Representative, Missouri State Legislature
Letter to Frank James

My Dear Frank,

To be succinct, yes, it is possible that the thing you describe can be gotten through the legislature. It will not be easy, and I cannot guarantee it. It may take some time, a year or more. It may be a full amnesty or it may not. You may even have to stand trial, be found guilty, and then pardoned. But there are still loyal men in the Party, and I believe we can count on them.

You have doubtless read or heard that General Keats is a partner in the syndicate that purchased one of the Kansas City papers. He is not only among them, Frank, he is chief among them, and, what's more, he has never forgotten how you saved him at Prairie Grove or what you and Jesse gave for your country.

This is what you must do. Have Jesse write a letter and send it to the editor of the Loyalist, care of Keats in Keatsville. If Jesse wants, I will write it for him, but I know, that with your help, he is more than capable of composing such a thing. But it must be Jesse who signs his name to it. He is young. He is handsome. His name rolls off the tongue like honey.

Tell him to proclaim his innocence. Tell him to remind the South of what he did for her. Loyal men will remember how the Yankees whipped him like a dog and hung his stepfather from a tree. Have him remind them of how he was shot down when he tried to surrender at war's end. Have him say that he will surrender again, but only if he is treated as a prisoner of war. Something along those lines.

That is how we must proceed. You and Jesse must raise a stir in your favor, whilst I work behind the scenes. Do nothing illegal. Stay low and stay quiet.

Yours, Through and Beyond Death,
Jax Brown

20

December 1873
Jesse James
Letter to The Kansas City Loyalist

Dillon, Montana, Dec. 25th
Dear Mr. Editor,

Will you please correct my composition and spelling and publish these words in your newspaper? You will see I never had the benefit of an education as it was cut short when a foreign power, which I need not name, invaded my country, and I was forced to take up arms to defend her.

Sometimes a few newspapers reach me in this far-flung place, and from those I see that me and my brother supposedly robbed a store in Cass County some weeks ago. We are likewise accused of robbing the train at Gads Hill, the Gallatin bank, the one at Ste. Genevieve, & some others over in Kentucky. But of all these crimes we are innocent, and anyone who is not a fool can see that we would need some sort of aerial ship in order to have carried out all the far-flung crimes of which we are accused.

I see also that we & Cole Younger are accused of robbing the fairgrounds at Kansas City and shooting down a little girl in making our escape. The men who did such a thing are poltroons, and I pray they are caught and dealt with severely.

I cannot speak for Younger, but I can say that neither I nor Frank were in Mo. when the fairgrounds was robbed & there are two dozen, loyal and true men who would testify to this.

Me & my brother would surrender today if we could be sure we would be treated fairly. We fought for our country during the war & when the end came I was shot down by militia while trying to surrender. Many men of Quantrill's and Howell's command have been dealt with by "Judge Lynch." But if we could stand trial without such circumstances occurring, then me and Frank could refute each and every charge brought against us.

Ask this, if you dare—what evidence, if any, do the Yankees and carpetbaggers have against us?

There is a horse that once belonged to me, but I can prove it was no longer mine when the Gallatin bank was robbed. And if some thief at the Fairgrounds says that his name is Jesse James, what proof is that? Anyone can say their name is Jesse James or Bobby Lee or Julius Caesar if they so please. Were I to rob a bank and say a name, I would not call myself Jesse James, but, instead, I would say I was Cole Younger, or some such a thing, to throw off the suspicion.

My brother & I do not like being in exile so far from home. But the Federals denied us our rights before, during, and after the war, and they deny them still. I only ask what is fair, and if what is fair is a bill of amnesty then I could have no objections to that.

Sincerely,
Jesse W. James

21
January 1874
Cole Younger
Letter to The Kansas City Loyalist

Dear Editor,

I have recently been mentioned in a certain letter written to and published by your newspaper, and I do not appreciate having my name bandied about with no thought to truth or honesty. I trust you will cease and desist from such practices.

I cannot say what may have prompted Mr. J. W. James to use my name in connection with the tragic robbery that occurred at the Kansas City Exposition almost two years ago, but I deny any knowledge of, or participation in, that awful event.

It is true that I was acquainted with Mr. James during the War for Southern Independence as the both of us were, for a time, at least, Partisan Rangers in the service of our country. I found him to be a likable, if somewhat reckless youth, but I have not seen Mr. James since 1863 when I quit the service of the Rangers.

After that date, I became a captain in the cavalry of Sidney Marion Keats who I served loyally and faithfully. When the surrender came I laid down my weapons, and since then I have tried to live in peace. I know there are some dangerous men roaming about the countryside, but I can only trust that the law will be vigilant and bring them to justice.

Sincerely,
Thomas Coleman Younger

22
March 1874
Billy Drury, Farmer
Clay County, Missouri

I was on my way home, one dark and lonely night, after spending a few days with my Uncle Benbow down in the Crackerneck. I'd left his place bright and early that morning, but Horace Greeley—my riding horse in those days—had a shoe come loose just as we reached the bridge over the Little Blue. I stopped at the tavern there to have the shoe tightened, but, like a fool, I dallied there too long debating the economic situation —there was a depression on, you see—with some of the ladies of the place.

We took a good three hours to conclude that this particular depression, like all others, was the fault of the Wall Street barons, the carpetbaggers, the "party of Grant" —that being the Republicans—the railroads, the banks, and, for some reason I cannot for the life of me recall, Mr. Charles Darwin. Still, it was a good time and a good debate, and, if you can remember the point of this digression, it's the reason Horace Greeley and I found ourselves on a lonely road in Jackson County, in the dead chill of night, with still two miles to go before the ferry.

The elms and sycamores crackled in the breeze. The clouds moved across the stars in phantom shapes. Yellow eyes watched from hiding places in the brush.

It's a well known fact—or used to be—that horses can see ghosts, which is what causes them to be as skitterish as they are. So, I was hunched over on Horace's back, looking between his ears, scanning the road ahead for apparitions, when I heard the jingle and snap of spurs and saddle leather coming towards me fast.

Not wanting to risk an encounter with mounted spooks, I called upon my woodsman's skills, pulled Horace into the brush, dismounted, and secreted myself among the hawthorn bushes.

I was just congratulating myself on my cleverness, when those ghostly riders stopped dead in front of where I was hiding.

"Billy. Billy Drury. That you in there?"

I stood up and showed myself. "Evenin' Frank," I said.

"What the hell are you doin', Billy. You'll get yourself killed creepin' around like that."

"Evenin' Jess," I said, leading Horace back into the road.

"Frank? Jesse?" Jess laughed. "Why, you mistake us for someone else."

He was about twenty-five or so years old by this time, and he wasn't any smooth cheeked innocent anymore. He pulled a flask out of his coat, took a big swig, then passed it on over to Frank.

"You do, indeed, mistake us," Frank said. "I don't know who you think we are, but it so happens we're Pinkerton detectives, and we just caught up with this miscreant here."

Frank pointed to the third member of the party, a young fellow, sitting atop a horse, bound, gagged, and looking very unhappy—a ghost soon to be, it turned out.

"He's a horse thief," Jess said, "and as bad as they come."

"A horse thief?" I said in disbelief.

Frank passed the flask down to where I stood, and I took a swig. Strong stuff, it was. I never thought Baptists were supposed to be drinkers, but that is how things go, I suppose— you rob a bank, kill a cashier or two, and before you know it, you're lost in the embrace of Mother Rum.

Jess said, "The damn fool's a Pinkerton. Just down from Chicago. Right boy?"

He looked at the fellow, and the fellow, gagged as he was, could only nod his head. A good looking young man he seemed to be, slender and neat in appearance.

"He's been poking around up at Mother's place," Jess said, "and we're going to teach him a lesson. Gonna dump him down here in Jackson somewhere. Make him walk back to Chicago."

He looked at the detective.

"That right boy?"

The detective nodded again, reminding me some of how Jess had looked during the war—wide-eyed and trembling.

"We're gonna take his clothes and boots," Frank said. "Dump him down here to make it look like Cole did it."

"Take his clothes," I said. "Well, that's a good one." I laughed. "Make him walk back to Chicago."

I laughed like I was getting a devil of a kick out of the whole situation, but that about dumping this detective in Jackson County, to make it look like Cole had done, it gave me pause.

Done what? I wondered. And wouldn't the detective himself know it was Frank and Jesse who'd kidnapped him and not the Youngers?

"Now, Jess," I began, "I hope you aren't meaning too..." But right then Jess went serious on me again.

"Jess?" he said. "Who's Jess?"

"Jess?" I said, playing along. "Is there someone round here named Jess?"

"You've got it right now, Billy," Jesse James said. He gave me a little salute, and him and Frank, with that poor detective in tow, rode off into a blackness of ghostly elms and wolf eyes.

When I got to the ferry—ten cents for people, twenty-five for horses—I had to rouse the ferryman, Bull Carter, a fellow who had chosen to shun human companionship for the most part. Usually, Bull wasn't too appreciative when a fellow woke him in the dead of night, but he was already up and didn't seem to mind.

"Already been across once tonight," he said. "Earlier on."

"Who did you carry?"

"Oh, just some fellows."

I pressed him. "What fellows would those be?"

"Detectives, they said they were. Did you see 'em on the road?"

"No," I said. "Didn't see a soul. Horace Greely threw a shoe. That's why I'm so late. Haven't see a soul since Little Blue Tavern."

Bull didn't believe me for a minute.

"Do you really think they'll let that boy go?"

"I doubt it," I said.

He thought a minute. "What'll we say if the law comes around?"

"I think it's best if we stay quiet."

"I think so, too," Bull Carter replied.

23

Spring 1874
William S. Beadle, Pioneer Photographer
Dodge City, Kansas

I have a tale to tell about Jesse James, but since so many have been told about him already, I shall first tell you the saga of one of those heroes who was truly responsible for The Winning of the West—me, William S. Beadle.

I was born in the east, of blue-blooded parents, in the year 1853 and lived a normal childhood. I went to school, played games and teased the girls. My heroes were the same ones most boys had—Boone, Crockett, Andy Jackson, the builders and ring-tailed roarers.

I was too young to fight for Abolition, but I would have if I could—Jackson would have, Boone and Crockett would have. A few years after the war ended, the westward surge of the American empire became the focus of my idealism. I was nineteen. The Great American Desert was just begging to be civilized, and I wanted to have a hand in it. But I was practical, too, and—realizing the west would be civilized by practical men—I began searching around for an occupation that would be useful in this new Promised Land.

For a time, I considered railroading. The nation was surging forward on iron wheels, after all, and the men who drove those steam leviathans were looked upon as gods.

Railroading might have been grand enough for me, but, unfortunately, I'd never been much of a physical specimen.

I thought for a time of going into banking or real estate. Men of commerce would be a necessity in bringing civilization to the wilderness. But just as often as such capitalists were idolized as builders, they were vilified as thieves, and William S. Beadle didn't want to go down in history classed as a Robber Baron.

It was then that I struck upon photography. Matthew Brady had done mankind and the nation a great service by recording the Civil War with his camera—not to mention gaining fame and fortune—and I supposed I could do the same by choosing The Winning of the West as a subject. Best of all, there didn't seem anything about photography that the common man couldn't master. I'd shot quail, after all, and photography didn't seem much different— you aimed the thing and pulled the trigger, that was all there was to it.

Armed with so fabulous an idea, I talked my father into lending—well, giving—me some money. I purchased hundreds of pounds of photographic equipment—whose functions I barely understood—and shipped the whole caboodle to St. Joseph, Missouri. I arrived there myself one spring morning, and immediately bought a wagon, mules, and supplies.

I cast myself adrift on the oceanic prairies in high spirits, but things went wrong in a hurry. First off, I took sick from eating spoiled bacon and, soon after, the prairie schooner some nice man had sold me at so reasonable a price began to shake itself to pieces on the plains of Kansas.

I made it into Dodge but no farther. The front axle broke right there on Division St.—by the old water tower—and, as I was pretty fed up by that time, I abandoned the wagon where she lay, sold the mules, fashioned a sign that proclaimed me a portrait artist, and wired home for more money.

My studio was the only such enterprise in Dodge, but I still had trouble scratching out a living. Dodge was a shipping point for buffalo hides, not cattle, in those days, and buffalo hunters didn't have much interest in portraiture. But in a few short years they'd managed to wipe out the buffalo—thereby starving out those same "backwards peoples" we'd intended to civilize—and the cowboy became king.

Kings, it seems, always require a portrait or two.

At the end of a day's work I was in the habit of relaxing for a few minutes by lounging in a chair on the sidewalk in front of my establishment, and taking in the only free entertainment to be had in town—watching the freights being switched in the yards on Front St.

One spring day, after work, I was sitting in peace, having a chat with one of my fellow empire builders, Squirrel Tooth Sally, her name was. That appellation didn't derive from any defect in her physical appearance, but, rather, from the fact that Sally loved squirrels and kept several as pets—she had a "sweet tooth for squirrels," so to speak.

Sally, in fact, was unusually pretty for a woman of her calling. She worked out of the Lady Gay—right across the street from my studio—dancing ten minutes with a man for seventy-five cents, then, if she was doing her job—which Sally always was—enticing him into her sleeping quarters in back.

"Oh, come now," she teased, as we relaxed in front of my studio. "I know you have the money. Taking people's portraits, why, I wish I had it that easy."

I fished into my coat pocket for my loose change, making as if I was totaling up my resources.

"I have a bit of cash," I said, "but not enough to interest Big Martha, much less you, Sally."

Sally laughed like a schoolgirl at that one.

"Oh, Bill. You do know how to charm a girl."

Sally and Martha, you see, had been mortal enemies since half-past December. Dodge had been snowed in most of that winter, and—during one cruel stretch when the girls hadn't set foot out of the Lady Gay for weeks—Martha, for no good reason, set fire to Sally's dress.

Pet squirrels to the contrary, Sally was no "hooker with a heart of gold." She always kept a small revolver tied to her wrist—but concealed in her purse or dress—and, when Martha set her aflame, Sally tried to pull it. But Martha beat her to the punch. Kicked her right in the chops, she did, and that was the end of it—hard girls, Sally and Martha.

Now, as we sat in front of my studio, Sally grew bored.

"Well," she said. "If you aren't willing to spend any money on me, why don't you take my portrait?"

"Oh, Sally," I replied, "you know I can't do you justice."

That was the truth. I must have taken a hundred pictures of Sally before she died—Sally with her squirrels in her lap, Sally with her pistol, Sally wearing the asafetida amulet she thought would keep her safe from fever. I never did manage to capture her, though.

It was right about then that a rider, heading for the toll bridge, trotted on past. Riders came and went in Dodge, so I paid this one no attention, but Sally jumped out of her seat.

"Jesse. Jesse," she cried. "Over here."

Upon hearing his name, the rider stopped short, looked over at us and began walking his horse in our direction. He carried three Smith & Wessons, a repeating rifle and a shotgun, besides, all of which was a bit much, even for Dodge. He had a beard that concealed most of his features, and, as he moved towards us, it occurred to me that he was a badman of one sort or another.

"Sally," he said. "What are you doing in an outpost like this?"

She shrugged her shoulders. "Just following the boom. You're a bit out of your territory yourself, aren't you?"

"Looking for some land," the badman replied. 'Lots of Texas boys around here, or so I hear."

He inclined his head towards the yellow quarantine flags that decorated a number of buildings.

"Town don't look healthy, though. Smallpox?"

"Cholera," Sally said.

I'd seen a thousand of this fellow's class since I'd come to Dodge, but this one struck me as a little brighter than your run of the mill bully. His features grew grim when cholera was mentioned, but his eyes never seemed to take a rest. They were always blinking or darting left and right, from one thing to another.

"My pa died of cholera, I think that's what it was."

"I know," Sally said. 'You told me before."

I didn't say a word through all this. It was clear to me that Sally liked this fellow, and I didn't like that at all. I had a bit of a crush on her, you see, and being caught between Sally and her admirers was not a new experience for me. But for once, I was determined not to exhibit any jealousy, so I just perched there, balancing my chair on its back legs.

"How's your ma doing?" Sally asked the badman.

"She's an old warhorse."

Not a very affectionate way to speak of one's mother, I thought, rocking back and forth.

"And Cole?"

"Cole's got a big head on him these days. I only see him on business."

Cole, I thought.

"And your brother? I think this is the first time I've seen you without him."

"Well..." The badman sighed. "He doesn't favor what I'm about to do. You know Frank," he laughed.

Frank, I thought. Cole, I thought.

"Jesse James," I blurted out. The words exploded from my mouth like a gunshot. Jesse's horse started. Susie went for her pistol, and I went over backwards in my chair, bang, onto the sidewalk.

The badman's eyes darted about like bumble bees. "Hold on there, friend. We don't want to go spreading any flying rumors, now. My name's Howard, Jesse Dave Howard. Call me Dave if you call me anything."

At that moment, a locomotive whistle screamed, and a freight, bound east, rumbled down Front Street casting black smoke and hot cinders in every direction—a hell of a town, Dodge. This occurrence, however, gave me time enough to pick myself up, regain my composure, and remember my role in The Winning of the West.

I'd taken the photographs of several notorious badmen—most of them in death—and "Dave's" would have been a fine portrait to add to my collection. I introduced myself, told him I was a photographer, and offered my services for free.

"For posterity's sake," I added.

"No," Dave replied. "It doesn't pay a fellow in my line of work to have his picture taken. But you may be of some help to me in another matter. I'm done with the rough life. Been thinking about settling somewhere, raising corn and children. I've found a good woman, and I think it's my best chance."

"Oh, Dave," Sally feigned a swoon, "you've always been so romantic."

Dave reached into the pocket of his coat, pulled out a letter and handed it down to her.

"You know the man who wrote that?" he said.

"No. No," Sally said, rather flustered.

Sally—though she'd entertained doctors, lawyers, congressmen and kings—couldn't read a line. She could recognize her name, a few words, maybe, but not much more.

"You know him, Bill?" she asked, passing the letter over to me.

"Well, let's see."

The letter was addressed to "Dave Howard, Keatsville, Mo." and had been sent by one of our local land brokers. Dodge, around this time, was becoming famous as a boom town, and certain men, in taking advantage of the publicity, were busy laying out new towns nearby—towns they never intended to actually build. These men would advertise the land in the eastern press—promising lots on the best sites—sell them by mail, then disappear with the proceeds.

But Dave, I gathered, wasn't about to buy a cat in a sack.

"I've heard of this fellow," I told him. "But I don't think he has many scruples."

"Well," said Dave, "Honest men have nothing to fear from me."

That remark struck me as a bit on the strange side, but I didn't have time to think about it. Sally, you see, couldn't stand being ignored, even for a minute.

"Come on," she said to Dave. "Let's go have a dance. Just for old times sake."

Dave shook his head. "I don't think so." He looked at me. "I'd best be moving on."

"Oh, don't be silly," Sally said. "We can have one little dance, now. Can't we? And you come too, Bill."

I shook my head. "I'm busy," I said.

The truth was, I'd watched her at work too many times before, and I wanted no more torture like that.

Sally gave us both that hurt look of hers—"Have it your way, then."

⌘

Sally didn't speak to me for about a week after that, and I was miserable the whole time. But that was her intent, I suppose, for I was something like one of those pet squirrels of hers— running round and round on a little wheel in my cage. I went crawling back to her, at last, but I won't recount much of the scene—embarrassing, it was. But I will tell you that I asked her how she could throw herself at a man like Jesse James.

"It's just commerce, Bill. It doesn't mean anything. He's an old friend from Fort Smith, that's all."

"A better friend than me, it seems."

"Oh, Bill."

I avoided Sally after that, because I just couldn't bear seeing her, anymore. We'd greet each other on the street, but I'd run off at the first excuse. After a while she started coming around to my studio.

"Remember me?" she'd ask, the little coquette.

We'd flirt on those occasions, and Sally would make joking propositions, just like always. But I didn't let it get me and soon after she stopped coming by altogether.

It was winter when Sally died—her kidneys, it was.

Big Martha came to visit her, along towards the end. She said her goodbyes and expressed apologies and regrets for the animosity they'd felt in the past—like people do when someone is dying. Everything seemed patched up between them, but as Martha turned to leave, Sally produced that little pistol of hers from under her pillow and shot Martha right in the ass. Never said a word, just shot her, bang, right in the ass.

I went on taking photographs—cowboys, babies, politicians, Chinamen, farmers and prize bulls—empire builders all.

As for the legends I photographed, well, those attempts were all somewhat disappointing. Bat Masterson looks more like a German immigrant than anything. His brother Jim looks like he's graduating high-school. But depicting legends, I now realize, is a job for Frederick Remington and his paint brushes, not William S. Beadle and his camera.

Remington could have shown Jesse James, you see. He could have painted a tall figure, mounted and riding through majestic, snowcapped mountains. He could have shown him as a tiny flyspeck, on an infinite plain, a heroic figure in a heroic land.

My camera would only have recorded a dull, somewhat disreputable looking fellow named Dave.

Squirrel Tooth Sally—I never even knew her last name. She worked hard, like most of us, did the best she could and ended up dead. She and Big Martha are both up on Boot Hill, now—the only two women so honored in Dodge. It's not much to show for a short, brutal life, but it's more than most of us empire builders end up with.

24
February 1875
THE NEW YORK EMPIRIC

THE JAMES GANG
—☆—

The Pinkerton's Attempt to Capture Them
Brave Acts of their Step-father
Aftermath of the Bombing

Yesterday, at midnight, two incendiary bombs were hurled through the back window of the family home of Frank and Jesse James, the notorious bandits of Missouri. One of these devices exploded, killed the James' nine year old step-brother, and wounded their mother.

At first, the Pinkerton National Detective Agency denied any knowledge of the affair, but the evidence that now presents itself seems otherwise.

For the past few months, members of the James Gang have dueled with Pinkertons on more than one occasion. These affrays resulted in the deaths of three detectives and of John Younger, brother of the notorious Coleman Younger, and it is thought that the Pinkerton's hatred of the Jameses was powerful enough to prompt them to attempt to get the outlaws by any and all means.

Yesterday, in the dark of night, a special train on the Hannibal & St. Jo line brought a large number of Pinkertons into Kearney, Missouri, the town that stands nearest the James' farm. Acting on information supplied by a spy working on the farm of a neighbor, these men made their way to the James' home, and hurled grenades into a room where innocents slept.

Dr. Reuben Samuel, Frank and Jesse's step-father, was awakened by the breaking of the glass and the cries of the Negro servants who slept in the kitchen. He rose from his bed in an adjoining room, came into the kitchen, and discovered an infernal device burning there. Thinking it a fire bomb, he and one of the Negroes swept it into the fireplace with a shovel.

As Dr. Samuel's wife and young son dashed in from the adjoining house, a second device was thrown into the kitchen. Dr. Samuel attempted to shovel this, too, into the fireplace, but, as he did, the first device exploded, felling his wife and the boy.

The noise of the explosion, and the sound of shots being fired, alerted a neighbor, Ralph Monroe. When he and others dashed to the scene, the Pinkertons fled like thieves in the night. While Mr. Monroe and the James' servants fought the fire that the explosion kindled, Dr. Samuel helped his wife to her bed and brought the wounded child to her.

"He lay his little head upon my face and kissed me," Mrs. Samuel said. "Then he noticed my wounds and said, 'Look at poor mama's arm.'"

These were the last words he ever spoke.

Dr. Tyler Stemp of Kearney was summoned, but the child had already expired. As part of Mrs. Samuel's right hand had been blown clear off, Dr. Stemp was forced to amputate up to the elbow.

Later, as she rested fitfully, Mrs. Samuel told our correspondent that all she wished for now was to see her two sons, Frank and Jesse, one last time before she died.

"I haven't seen them in almost a year. Is that too much for an old woman to ask?"

Despite Mrs. Samuel's statement, there is at least some evidence that points to the presence of one or both of her sons on the night of the bombing. There are bullet holes in the fence, tracks in the snow, and spent cartridges all around, making it appear as if a gunfight of some sort had indeed taken place. Curious also, is the fact that, sometime after Dr. Stemp's arrival, his horse disappeared from the barn. It was later found three miles away, having been hard ridden, and the most accepted explanation is that either Frank or Jesse were hiding inside the house through the whole affair, and, later, used the doctor's animal for escape.

Still, the death of the child has engendered much sympathy for the James in these parts. Newspapers that were heretofore against them, now say that the Pinkerton's actions were barbarous.

Detective P. P. Ferris of the Pinkerton's St. Louis office, claimed that all such talk is ridiculous.

"The bomb that was thrown was intended to smoke the Jameses out and nothing more," he said. "It exploded only because of the flames in the fireplace."

Angered, he asked our correspondent, "And how many innocents have the Jameses killed in the course of their depredations? Why don't you go and interview some of the orphans they've made? Go and speak with the widow of the engineer who was killed when they wrecked the train at Turkey Creek. Ask her children what they think of Jesse James."

25

Spring 1875
Jesse James
Letter to The Kansas City Loyalist

Winnemucca, Nevada
Dear Mr. Editor,

For years, Billy Pinkerton of Chicago has accused me and my brother of almost every crime committed in the whole of the country. But look at the facts. My dear wife & I have been living in this barren desert ever since we were married, and my brother has been living in Juarez, Mexico, for an even longer time.

Billy Pink & his lackeys were spies for the north during the war, and they have never forgiven us for having the courage of our convictions. They cannot prove that I have ever harmed anyone, but they cannot deny that they threw a bomb into a house full of innocents, maimed a poor, old, gray-haired mother, and murdered a boy who had not yet shaved.

The Pinkertons line their pockets with more stolen lucre than a highwayman could ever dream of, and now it has been proved that Grant's campaign chest was filled by the whiskey distillers of St. Louis. What justice is there in this?

My brother says that Grant and the Republicans will not withdraw their armies of occupation from the South for a thousand years, and I believe him. Such tyrants as Grant were once curbed by the *fear of rebellion, but they are no longer. They quell the mob by telling them to speak at the polls, but it is lying newspapers like The St. Louis Union that tell the people how to vote, and it is Pinkertons who count the ballots.*

I am not wise enough to know how the South can free itself from Grant's iron grip so I have followed the words of the Bible which tells us we should turn the other cheek. For ten long & brutal years, I have done so, but now I see some hope for us, as there is a bill of amnesty introduced in the Missouri legislature, by Colonel Jax Brown, which would, once and forever, end the persecution of the Jameses.

If this bill were put to the people, and the vote were to be counted fairly, I have no doubts as to the outcome. But there are many men in the legislature who are on Grant's payroll, and I fear they will be forced to vote for more persecution.

My dear wife & I married for love & because we wanted children. She is about to bear our first child, and we pray that the many good, Democratic men left in the legislature, will not be deluded by the lies & deceptions of Billy Pinkerton and his ilk. Our fondest wish is that our baby will be born and raised in Missouri, and my wife and I urge all the representatives, for the sake of the unborn if no other, to vote aye when the amnesty comes up before them.

Sincerely,
Jesse W. James.

26

October 1875
Billy Drury, Farmer
Clay County, Missouri

One night I was at home, like always, sitting by the stove minding my own business. It was raining outside and the wind was blowing so hard I'd had to tie the chickens down to keep 'em from being swept away. Then, just as I was thinking of laying my weary bones down for the night, I heard a voice outside.

"Hello, Billy. You in there?"

I opened the door and there was Jesse James in a long, rain slicker looking wet, bedraggled, and desperate.

"Well, ho, Jess," I said, doing my best to conceal my true feelings. "Come on in and make yourself comfortable."

I told him to put his horse in the barn, and he said he already had. He was carrying a small valise in one hand and a Winchester rifle, still in its saddle scabbard, in the other. He took off his slicker, went over by the stove and stood there warming his backside.

"How've you been, Billy?"

"You know me. Can't complain. How's your mother doin'?"

"Oh, not to bad, under the circumstances."

"How're things with you and the wife?"

"Oh, I got her stuck away up in Kentucky or somewheres."

He grinned like the cat who'd ate the canary. "I'm going to be a papa, Billy."

"A papa. Why that's just something, Jess."

"Did you see I'm front page news again?"

"No," I said, "I suppose I don't get much chance to see the papers."

"And it's not just the Kansas City papers, or even the ones in St. Louis. I'm front page news in New York City, Billy."

He moved over to that wet slicker of his, reached into one of the pockets, and pulled out a little package all wrapped up in oilskin.

"Take a look here."

He had a good two-dozen newspaper articles in that oilskin, and he got 'em out and passed 'em to me.

"According to those," he laughed, "I'm to blame for that uprising in Vicksburg."

"No," I said.

Right about that time, some white folks in Vicksburg had attacked the courthouse and strung up some carpetbaggers. Jesse hadn't had anything to do with that, of course—no profit in lynching carpetbaggers.

"My enemies are scared to death this amnesty will go through," he said. "They'll tell any lie about me."

"I sure hope it works out for you," I said. The bill was in the legislature as we spoke—an amnesty for Frank and Jesse and all their misunderstood, murdering friends.

"Of course," he said, "there's a chance I might have to stand trial for something or another, even if the amnesty goes through, but I believe I can count on my friends."

Then those steely eyes of his fell right on me.

"Billy," said Jesse James. "You remember that night a couple years ago, when you met some fellows on the road near the ferry?"

"Well, yes. I suppose I do."

I chose my words with care because Frank and Jesse had murdered that poor detective they'd captured that night. They'd told me they were just going to steal his clothes and let him go, but they'd lied.

Worse, still, to my way of thinking, it wasn't a murder done in battle or in some desperate flight from the scene of a crime. Frank and Jesse had made that detective get off his horse and, while he pleaded for his life, most likely, they'd shot him down in cold blood—once in the heart and once in the head.

"What I mean to say," I told Jess, "was that I chanced to meet some detectives one night who'd captured a horse thief."

"We didn't kill that boy." Jesse shook his head. "It was the Youngers who did it. We let that boy go down in Jackson, just like we'd said. The Youngers found him and killed him. They tried to make it look like we did it. Cole's always been against me, you know."

"Never did trust Cole, myself," I said, which was the truth. Never did trust Jess, either, but I didn't say so.

And, who knows? It could have been the Youngers that did it. They just could have been riding around the countryside in the dead of night. They just might have chanced upon that detective, somewhere, after Frank and Jesse had dropped him off. Or it could have been a band of wild Apaches. Or maybe Attila the Hun had been in the neighborhood, for that matter.

Then, all of a sudden, Jess up and asked me if I had a saw.

"A good one," he added, "no rust, but clean and bright."

"I should say I got a saw," I said. "I should say there ain't a farmer in Missouri ain't got a saw."

"Would you mind gettin' it for me? If it ain't too much trouble?"

The saw was out in the barn, the rain was coming down like the devil, and the wind was blowing the chickens from here to Kingdom Come.

"No, no. No trouble at all, Jess."

I got into my overcoat and boots and put on my rain hat and went out to the barn wondering all the time, what in the name of all creation Jesse James could be wanting with a saw. Then, it came to me.

If Jess had to stand trial, I realized, I'd be called on to testify against him, and it was only me and Bull Carter, the

131

ferryman, who knew the truth behind that detective's death. Jess, I figured, feared I'd spill the beans, and he meant to shoot me dead and cut my body up with my own saw.

Such a thought may seem comical now, but it wasn't then. Jesse James had murdered a twenty year old detective, in cold blood, after all. He'd killed bank clerks, cashiers, and innocent bystanders in the course of his depredations. I didn't suppose he'd flinch from murdering some useless, old bastard like me.

When I got to the barn, I considered making a run for it. My horse was there. His horse was there. I could have been gone with both of them before he knew the difference, but my hands were already trembling, and it wouldn't have been easy, getting a saddle and bridle on Horace Greeley in that condition. And what if Jess got suspicious? What if he came and found me, just as I was about to ride out? And how far would I get with the James Gang on my trail? Fifty-five years old, I was, and not as spry as I'd once been.

"Looks like a nice one," Jesse said, when I got back with the saw. He flexed the blade with his hands. "Billy, I'm gonna show you a little trick I picked up down in Arkansas." He reached for his rifle scabbard, and I thought my time was up.

But instead of pulling out his weapon, he pulled out a goddamned fiddle bow and right there, in the middle of my kitchen, Jesse James sat down, stuck the handle of that saw between his knees, bent the end of it with his left hand, and ran the bow across it with his right.

"What's your favorite song, Billy?" he said.

My heart was pounding. Boom. Boom. Boom.

"Well," I blurted out. "I suppose I've always been partial to 'My Grandfather's Clock.'" That's the one that goes, "My grandfather's clock set and ticked on the shelf, til the old buzzard died," or some such.

"Well." He scratched his beard. "That ain't a real good saw tune. How would you feel about 'Sweet Genevieve?'"

I told him that would be fine, and he started tapping his foot, then launched into it, "Sweet Genevieve"—a melancholy and sentimental lament, concerning things lost and the way they might have been. It was no "Grandfather's Clock," I'll say, but Jess did a workman like job on it. He strung out the long notes and laid on a lot of tremolo. He stopped and started over, once or twice, but played fine, on the whole.

Then, however, he commenced bellowing.

"'My Genevieve, Sweet Genevieve. The days may come, the days may go. But still the hands of mem-'ry weave, the blissful dreams of long ago.'"

It was awful, and I realized a little liquor was what was needed. As I poured us out a couple of cups, Jess took a breather and asked me how my cousin was getting on.

"Which cousin?" I said—had about four million of them.

"Julia Fanning, up in Monrovia. Feisty little pup, she was. Had a temper almost as bad as mine. Threw me out of her house one night during the war. I was young and a fool in those days."

"She's Julia Fanning Breckenridge now," I informed him. "Lives down in Alabama, surrounded by luxury, or so I understand."

"Married a Breckenridge, did she? Well, more power to her. Anything else you'd like to hear?"

"Well," I said. "How 'bout 'Am I A Soldier of the Cross?'" I knew that was always a favorite of his.

"That's a real back breaker," Jess said. "Truth is, the only tune I've really learned proper is 'Sweet Genevieve.'"

"Well, then, 'Sweet Genevieve,' it is."

I don't know if the liquor made Jess sing better after that, or if it just made me think he was singing better.

"'For me the past has no regret. Whatever the years may bring to me. I bless the hour when we first met. The hour that gave me love and thee.'"

Before I knew it, I found myself singing along on the chorus.

"'Oh Genevieve, Sweet Genevieve. The days may come, the days may go...'"

We drank some more liquor and sang "Sweet Genevieve" a good ten hundred times, the tears streaming down our cheeks. It was a mournful exhibition, I suppose, and then, without warning, Jess started coughing.

Deep down coughs, they were, from the depths of his lungs. His whole body shook from them, and he got up and went to the door. He opened it, braced himself against the wall, coughed up all sorts of ugliness from deep down inside, and spit it out into the rain.

When he stepped back inside he allowed as how he was all played out.

"I guess I've done enough singing for one night," he said. He flexed the fingers on his right hand. "And I'm starting to stiffen up. It don't pay to have a stiff hand in my line of work."

He laughed. "Did you hear they found a big deposit of coal on one of General Keats' farms, over in Ray County?"

"I heard," I said. "Don't seem fair."

"Well, money comes to money." He shrugged his shoulders. "He's just one of those fellows who could fall down the outhouse well and come up smelling of roses...You got any laudanum, Billy?"

The next morning, I woke rather late and with a miserable and pounding headache. Jess was already gone, but he'd left two dollars on the table, just like always, to pay for his board.

In the years since, I've sometimes wondered whether Jesse James could have given up the outlaw life even if that amnesty had gone through. Murder and pillage are hard habits for a man to break, I suppose. Still, even Jess must have wondered, a time or two, what might have happened if it had. Who knows, maybe he'd have become what he was always meant to become —a farmer raising corn and children. Or maybe he would have devoted his life to the musical saw—no man has ever truly mastered that instrument, or so a banjo player once told me.

Any man can succeed in this life if he works hard, or so they say. But I won't pass judgment. No, I'll leave that to the politicians and editorial cartoonists. I'm just a farmer, after all, and not a very good one at that.

27

September 1876
Texas John Overstreet, Pinkerton Detective
Denver, Colorado

The whole truth will never be known—all the witnesses are either lying or dead—but there's a story going round that says Jesse James turned coward after the Northfield robbery.

I imagine every red-blooded boy in the nation knows the story of that ill-fated raid—how the James Gang went all the way to Northfield, Minnesota, to rob a bank and got shot up bad as they made their escape. Two of the gang's lesser lights died right outside the bank, and every one of them was wounded.

Jim Younger had a bullet in his shoulder and, during the long pursuit that followed the robbery, his wound became infected. He was feverish. He'd lost a lot of blood. The posses were hot on their heels.

"None of us will make it with Jim slowing us down," Jesse James told Cole Younger.

"We can't leave him behind," Cole said.

The night was black and moonless. The rain pelted down. Storms had turned the world into a sea of mud, and the gang couldn't even risk the comfort of a fire.

"We're guerrilla fighters, Cole. You know what we have to do."

Jesse's defenders, as you might expect, say the whole tale is false from top to bottom. They say Jesse never wanted to kill Jim and I admit that I don't know for certain what happened that night. But I was among the party of hunters who captured the Youngers, three days after the alleged incident, and I can tell you that parts of the tale have an uncanny accuracy about them.

When we captured Jim Younger, he was in as bad a shape as any man I've ever seen. He'd taken another bullet—this in the jaw—when we'd shot it out with the gang and, when we found him, he was lying in the mud, half unconscious, covered with blood and filth.

My partner, Captain P. P. Ferris—"Monk" we called him—took one look at Jim and said, "You won't live long enough to hang."

Cole Younger lay near his brother with six bullets in him. Monk knelt down beside him.

"Where's Jesse?"

Cole spit right in his eye. "Piss on you."

But Monk ended up getting the last laugh. The gang had been on foot for several days, you see, and Cole had made the mistake of wearing stylish boots instead of practical ones. When those wore out, he'd wrapped rags around his bare feet and, now, the rags were stuck to his skin.

As we lifted Cole into a wagon, Monk took one look at those rags—stiff with blood and mud—and said they had to come off.

"Infection," Monk said. "Gangrene. Who knows what's under there."

Monk pulled the rags off, one by one, and Cole's toenails came off with them. He bellowed in pain every time Monk ripped off a rag and a nail.

"Piss on you," Cole screamed.

Monk just laughed.

⌘

I was pretty green on that manhunt—eighteen years old was all. Six months before, I'd been working as a bellboy in the St. James Hotel in St. Louis, Missouri. Monk was one of the high rollers who used to lounge around the lobby there, and I can see him even now, sitting in an easy chair, smoking a big cigar, flicking the ashes into a potted palm.

Whenever I got the chance, I bragged to him about my exploits. I'd been a cowboy before coming to St. Louis, but down in Galveston I'd gotten into a dispute over the ownership of some mavericks with a certain son of a bitch named Ainsmith.

"I'd be in Texas, still," I told Monk, "if he hadn't hired a gunman to chase me."

Monk just nodded his head. "If you're as rough as you say you are, you ought to come round and see us. The Pinkerton Agency is always on the lookout for rough boys."

I told him no thank you.

"I'm making better money as a bellboy than the Pinks pay. This job is plush, and I won't have anything to do with Yankees."

I was too young to remember the war very well. But I knew the Pinkertons had spied for the north, and my principles put me above working for them—or so I thought.

But not a month later, I got into a fight with the head bellboy over tips, and my plush job went right out the window. When I first came to St. Louis, I'd lived on the streets. I didn't want to go back to that, so I decided to join the Pinks afterall— so much for my principles.

On my first assignment, I worked undercover at the International Hotel trying to determine who'd been stealing the silverware. It wasn't what I'd had in mind when I joined up, but I got my man, all right.

Not long after, a telegram arrived from Mr. Allen Pinkerton in Chicago, the "Big Eye" himself, and all the agents gathered round as Monk studied it.

"The Jameses have robbed a bank in Minnesota," he said. "The Eye is bringing in men from all over. He wants two from here. I'm one. Who's going with me?"

Everyone spoke up, but Monk's big eyes fell on me. Heavy eyes they were, with thick brows that stood out like—well—like a monkey's.

"What about it, Texas? Are you rough enough to tangle with Jesse James?"

Nobody had ever called me Texas before, and I rather liked it.

"You know I am," I said.

The two of us rode an express from St. Louis to Chicago, then connected with a local that dropped us in Mankato, Minnesota. The town was bursting with lawmen. A vast net was being thrown across the James's probable line of retreat, and every man among us was intent on having the honor of killing or capturing Frank and Jesse.

Monk and I were ordered to take two Mankato men and search west, towards Madelia, where the Jameses had been spotted two days before. As we prepared to move out, Monk wrapped canvas leggings around his calves—from the tops of his boots to the bottoms of his knees.

"It's a fool trick to send us to Madelia," I told him. "The trail is as frigid as a nun."

Monk just shrugged. "You ought to be looking after your gear, Texas. It's going to be wet out there."

"I got rained on plenty of times when I was a cowboy. It's like water off a duck's back."

Monk didn't say a word.

The day after we left Mankato, we interviewed a hog farmer who told us that six men, two riding double, had come by his place the morning before. They'd been dressed in fashionable, long slickers—of the type worn by cattle buyers—but they were filthy and bloodstained.

One man, the farmer told us, had a wet bandage across his right eye. That man, I believe, was Jesse James. The one who did the talking had a bullet hole in his left leg—that was Frank.

"The name's Woods," Frank told the hog farmer. "We're detectives, chasing the blackguards who robbed the Northfield bank. You haven't seen them, have you?"

The hog farmer said he hadn't seen a thing.

"You wouldn't have any horses you'd like to sell, would you?"

The hog farmer said he didn't.

"Well, you look plump enough, you must have some food around."

The farmer sold them some bread and butter, and as they wolfed it down, they asked directions. The farmer told them which way to go, but when they rode off, they went back in the direction they'd just come from. That information seemed mysterious to us at the time, but the fact was that the legendary James Gang was lost and riding in circles.

The rains started soon after and, before long, traveling got so hard we made camp. That was when Monk got me for how I'd bragged in Mankato.

"Since you're such a Texas duck," he said, "why don't you stand watch tonight?"

I didn't like the idea of spending the night with nothing but a slicker for cover, but I was a young fool and wasn't about to show Monk any weakness. Instead, I went over to my pack, pulled out a jar of brandied peaches I'd bought in Mankato— don't ask me why—and sauntered over to a position by the road. I pulled my slicker up over my head, squatted down in the wet, and began eating those damn peaches like I was loving every minute of it.

⌘

Jesse and his gang, it turned out, were camped not more than four miles away from us that night. People say they huddled under their rain slickers, just like me.

"If this keeps up," Jesse is supposed to have said, "we'll be in mud to our knees."

"We've dodged posses before," Cole Younger replied.

"None of us will make it with Jim slowing us down."

"You won't make it," Cole said, "if you don't shut up."

"We're guerrilla fighters. You know what we have to do, and you're the one to do it."

"I won't do any such thing."

Jesse drew his pistol.

"Are you with me, Frank?"

"I'm always ready to stand by my little brother," Frank said. He went over to Jesse, took out his own pistol, and pointed it at Cole and Bob Younger.

"I'll keep these misfits at bay while you dispatch their weaker sister."

Jesse turned towards Jim—cool and calm, perhaps, or nervous and trembling, maybe. Cole and Bob shouted in protest. Jesse raised his pistol. But before he got it on the level, Frank brought his own shooting iron down on Jesse's skull and cold-cocked him.

Thunk!

"I'm sorry for this, Cole," Frank said, as Jesse lay in the mud before them.

"Guerrilla fighters. Good God. We're bank robbers. The damn boy has lost his marbles."

"You'd better get him out of here," Cole said, "or he'll lose more than that. I'll kill the son of a bitch if I ever see him again."

⌘

I don't know if that was how it happened or not, but the next morning it was raining even worse—I know that. Monk and I and the Mankato men broke camp and, soon after, we met another party that was hunting the Jameses. It was under the command of a sheriff from Gridley. I don't remember his name, but we joined forces with them, meaning there were nine of us, now.

That night, the rain let up long enough for us to build a fire out of wet wood, but, still, Monk woke up with a cold the next morning. I thought that was pretty funny until I started sneezing, too.

Around noon, we saw some men gnawing raw turnips in a turnip patch. Monk put his spyglass on them, but before we could close in, another party of hunters, these with dogs, came up and scared them off.

Monk was furious and laid into them.

"Goddamn amateurs," he said.

Later, we fought a running gun-battle with the robbers—there were about twenty of us now—until, at last, we cornered them between the junction of two rivers at a place called Hanska Slough.

Monk called out to them and demanded they surrender.

"You sons of bitches of Pinkertons," came the reply. "You come in and get us."

Monk decided we should form a skirmish line and advance toward the river at the walk. It took us a few minutes to assemble, then Monk shouted out the order to advance and we all raised up and began firing.

Monk and I were in the center of the line, and, by now, the outlaw's return fire was so sporadic I advanced without a thought to my own safety. Then, one of them jumped out of the brush in front of me and fired a bullet that shattered my left forearm.

Monk fired at the same time and the man fell down dead. Then another of the outlaws—Bob Younger—stood up in his hiding place, threw down his gun, and raised his hands.

"Don't shoot anymore. I'm the last one left."

Monk walked over to the man he'd just killed and examined him.

"I don't think he's anybody important," Monk said, disappointed that it wasn't Jesse or Frank. He took a look at my arm where I'd been hit.

"The bone's sticking out, but you might not die."

"It doesn't hurt much."

"You're a rough boy, Texas."

Monk had tied cords around his slicker at the elbows to keep the sleeves from getting in his way and, now, he undid one of them and made a tourniquet for me. By this time, the sheriff from Gridley had found the other two Younger brothers, shot up and lying in the brush.

"You won't live long enough to hang," Monk told Jim Younger.

"Where's Jesse?" he said to Cole.

"Piss on you," Cole spat.

The sheriff shackled Bob Younger, and Bob asked Monk if he had any dry matches. Monk gave him one and all of us lit up a smoke.

"Where's Jesse?" Monk said.

"We split up two days ago," Bob told him. "The son of bitch abandoned us."

"You're lying. Where's he hiding?"

"It better not be around here," Bob said.

He was just about to spill the proverbial beans, when Cole shouted out an order.

"Don't tell the damn bastards anything. Piss on 'em. Make 'em work for their blood money."

Monk and I tried to pump Bob some more, but, after that, it wasn't any use. His brother had told him to shut up and shut up he had.

About that time, the sheriff from Gridley procured a spring wagon from a nearby farm, and we loaded it with the dead and wounded.

Monk told me to ride in the wagon, but I objected.

"You've proved you're a rough boy, Texas, now quit being an ass and get in the wagon."

That settled that.

⌘

Monk Ferris chased Jesse James half his life but never did catch up with him. A few years later, he came close. We surrounded Jack Doyle, a later recruit of Jesse's, in an oyster bar just outside Nashville. But Doyle was a rough boy, too, and, before surrendering, he managed to put a bullet into Monk's abdomen.

I visited Monk every day in the hospital after he was shot. His wife was always there. I didn't think his wound was mortal, but it got infected. Monk lingered and lingered and fought and fought, but finally gave up the ghost as his poor wife watched and wept.

The dime novel writers like to turn lawmen, like Monk and me, into villains. They turn murderers, like Jesse, into heroes, but I don't think even they believe that sort of tripe. If someone steals their money, they yell for the Pinks or the coppers, not Mr. Jesse James.

Jesse's defenders can say all they want about how brave and loyal he was. But at Northfield, him and his gang murdered the bank cashier and killed an innocent bystander to boot—a wife and three children, the cashier left behind. And on that same rainy night I ate that jar of brandied peaches, the great man, Jesse James, betrayed his friends. That's what I think, at any rate. You can think whatever you want.

28
October 1876
THE PHILADELPHIA ILLUSTRATED WEEKLY
General Sidney Marion Keats
Famed Confederate Calvary Leader
Visits the Centennial Exposition

— ☆ —

His Thoughts on the Missouri Bandits
His Political Ambitions

The celebrated Confederate cavalry leader, Sidney Marion Keats, has been in Philadelphia these last few days, taking in the wonders of the Centennial Exposition. The General, who failed in his bid for the Democratic nomination in the Missouri gubernatorial race two years ago, was in the company of his long time friend and associate, Colonel J. A. X. Brown. Colonel Brown, who is now a representative in the Missouri legislature, attained notoriety at war's end, when he refused to surrender to the Union and, instead, led his troops to Mexico.

Our reporter interviewed the two gentlemen last Thursday, as they dined with family and friends at the Exposition's fabulously acquitted French restaurant, the Trois Freres Provencaux.

Reporter: "General Keats, what is your reaction, thus far, to our glorious Exposition?"

Gen. Keats: "I can hardly claim to have seen it in its entirety, but during my visit I have been especially impressed by American Industry. The North seems to lead all other nations in machinery, invention, and progress. The South would do well to follow its lead."

Reporter: "And how do you find the food of France this evening?"

144

Gen. Keats: "It's extortion, I think, to charge a man extra for rolls and butter."

Reporter: "It's our understanding that, during the war, you befriended both Frank and Jesse James, the notorious outlaws."

Gen. Keats: "Yes. Bands of Partisan Rangers were grouped under me, and I'm proud to number among my friends, certain men who offered to sacrifice their lives in defense of their country."

Reporter: "And have you seen Frank and Jesse since they turned to a life of crime?"

Gen. Keats: "Hold on there, young man. The Jameses have been mentioned in the press as being involved in certain acts, but never once have accusations been made by responsible witnesses in front of a jury. Are not men still presumed innocent in this country?"

Reporter: "There are rumors to the effect that the Jameses were killed sometime during, or after, the recent Northfield, Minnesota, bank robbery. Have you seen or heard from them since then?"

Gen. Keats: "That is just the sort of thing I've been talking about. There is not a scrap of evidence to the effect that the Jameses were involved in the Northfield raid at all and, now, you say they were killed there. It's ridiculous."

Reporter: "But it is common knowledge, is it not, that the Jameses and Youngers ride together? The Youngers, since their capture, have confessed to the robbery, so is it not reasonable to wonder if the Jameses might have been there too?"

Col. Brown: "You're a lazy boy, aren't you? If you weren't, you'd have taken the trouble to have read the Younger's confession, and if you had, you'd know they never once implicated the Jameses."

Reporter: "Actually, sir, I have read the Younger's confession, but I wonder if it can be wholly believed? The Youngers have been charged with murder, afterall, and Minnesota doesn't hang men who confess. Don't you suspect they might have been more interested in avoiding the noose than telling the truth?"

Gen. Keats: "And what of it? You'd want to avoid such a thing, wouldn't you? I think any man would."

Col. Brown: "What the General means to say is that Minnesota law is wholly irrelevant in regards to the Younger's reasons for confessing. I've spoken with them since their capture, and they're truly repentant of what they did."

145

Gen. Keats: "Precisely. And, in defense of the Youngers, I would add that the Northfield raid was the only so-called crime they ever committed."

Reporter: "Then why do you suppose officials of the law and hundreds of detectives have been tracking them all these years?"

Gen. Keats: "For that answer you should ask men in higher places than I."

Reporter: "And what men would those be?"

Gen. Keats: "You know who I mean. Go ask a carpetbagger."

Reporter: "Do you mean to say there are certain highly placed officials who would knowingly accuse innocent men of crimes in order to serve some devious end?"

Gen. Keats: "I came here to eat dinner, not to be badgered. I'm a cavalry man, not a politician. Ask me about cavalry."

Reporter: "In that case, would you care to comment on the tactics of Col. Custer in the tragic massacre of last July?"

Gen. Keats: "I lay the blame entirely at the feet of the Republicans. Millions have been appropriated for the purpose of civilizing the Indians, but I doubt the money ever arrived in the hands of those it was intended for. And, even if it did, well then, the Custer business would force one to conclude it had all been wasted."

Reporter: "Since we seem to have strayed back into the political arena, General, perhaps you would be so kind as to tell us if you will again seek the Democratic nomination for governor of Missouri, two years hence."

Gen. Keats: "I seek nothing. But I am a loyal, party man, and if my party calls, I will do what is necessary."

Reporter: "Thank you, gentlemen, for your patience."

Gen. Keats: "It was nothing."

29

Spring 1877
Mrs. W. H. L. Pemberton, Bookkeeper, Pemberton Feed
& Grain
Nashville, Tennessee

Wilton, my husband, didn't have a head for business so I always kept an eye on him.

One day he was up at the front counter—I could watch him from my desk in back—having a long and animated conversation with a man I'd never seen before—a good looking fellow with a full, black beard that hid most of his features.

"I was with Bragg," I heard Wilton say, "at Chickamaugua and Lookout Mountain."

"If the armies were to march tomorrow," the handsome man said, "I'd be marching with them."

When they shook hands and grinned like school chums, I grew suspicious. I went out to the loading dock and, as I feared, a wagon drawn by two, big mules was being loaded down with a dozen bales of alfalfa and two score sacks of high grade oats. I asked one of the porters who it was for.

"Why that man, ma'm." He inclined his head towards the handsome gentleman I'd seen inside. "Mr. Howard, his name is."

"We'll see about that."

"Yes, ma'm."

Don't misunderstand me, Wilton was a good man—loyal, honest, and hard working—but not very progressive. Nashville was being reborn in the seventies and industry and commerce boomed. Huge tracts of farmland were being put under development and houses sprung up like weeds. In such an environment, business could no longer be conducted on the basis of family, friendship and a handshake, but Wilton could never understand that.

"I hope you didn't extend that fellow any credit," I said when I was back inside. I'd taught school before marrying Wilton and, whenever I confronted him, I always assumed my most terrifying schoolteacher's voice.

"I've told you before, and I'll tell you again, never give a man credit unless you know something about him."

"But I do know something about him, dear. His name is John Davis Howard and he's from Arkansas. He's rented a little farm, just outside town, and he intends to raise horses and run some cattle."

"And he fought for the South, I suppose."

"Yes, he fought for the South. He was a cavalryman."

"Everyone was a cavalryman, or so it would seem from your acquaintances. And you've given that fellow enough feed for a whole regiment. I know how terrible the war was. I know how you feel about it. But we just can't extend credit to men we've never seen before."

"But I have seen him before."

"And just where did you see him?"

"In church."

"Church? Our church? I've never seen him in church. Where was I when you supposedly saw him in our church?"

"In bed, asleep."

I needed my rest on Sundays, but only because I worked so hard during the week. I'm sure the Lord would have understood that. But, when my husband finally fessed up and admitted that he had not only given this J. D. Howard credit, but had also loaned him three hundred dollars straight up—no contract, no signatures, just a handshake—well, I was forced to look a little deeper into Mr. Howard's character.

On the Sabbath, following, I struggled out of bed, dressed up in my best and accompanied Wilton to Grace Methodist— where we always paid our tithing on time and were members in good standing.

"Well, where is he?" I said, as we settled in the pews.

"You just wait, dear, he'll be here." Wilton pulled a hymnal from the back of the pew in front of us and pawed through it, feigning interest.

"The service is about to start," I said, as the choir filed in. "If your Mr. Howard intends to be here on time, he'll be hard pressed. It's always so embarrassing when someone walks in late and disrupts the service."

"Have a look over there." Wilton lifted a finger off his hymnal and pointed discretely at the choir.

"Well, glory be."

Mr. Howard—all decked out in a long, black, choir robe— walked in with the rest of them—in perfect silence, his eyes downcast. He took his place in the back row, amongst the baritones and again, I was struck by how handsome he looked. His eyes were what interested me most—steely blue, they were, with a gun metal gleam, I'm tempted to say.

"Did I tell you he also helps teach the Sunday school?" Wilton said.

"You know very well you didn't."

The subject of Reverend Bird's sermon that day was "Judge Not Lest Ye Be Judged," and Wilton poked me in the side all through it.

"You stop that now."

"Stop what, dear?"

Later, Mr. Howard carried off a brief solo during the choir's singing of "Am I a Soldier of the Cross" with enthusiasm and courage if not consummate skill. Afterwards, we refreshed ourselves with cookies and tea in the day room— the cookies were shortbread and simple, but the tea was hot. Wilton dragged me to where Mr. Howard stood.

"My wife was much impressed by your singing," Wilton told him.

"Why thank you, Mrs. Pemberton." Howard smiled his handsomest smile. "I don't really do the singing, ma'm. Half of it is the Lord. The other half is sheer bluff."

"My husband tells me you raise horses. Are they intended for riding, or are they more along the lines of Morgans and Percherons?"

"Well, no, ma'm. They're riding horses. At least, after a fashion."

"And just what is a horse 'after a fashion?'"

"They're race horses, ma'm."

"Race horses?" I looked at Wilton. "You mean we're backing race horses?"

Wilton tried to shrug it off. "I wouldn't say 'backing them,' exactly."

"Don't worry, Mrs. Pemberton," Howard said. "When I ride a race there's no gambling involved. I learned my horsemanship from Quantrill and Bub Howell. There have never been riders such as they, and there will never be again."

Despite my misgivings, Wilton continued doing business with J. D. Howard, extending him more credit and, I fear, lending him more money. But I didn't have occasion to converse with the gentleman again until later that summer, when we attended the State Fair—which we always did in order to advertise our establishment and keep up with the latest developments.

One afternoon, after traipsing through livestock exhibits all morning, Wilton and I rested our weary feet in the Breeder's Club, which was not only suitable for ladies, but also had a fine view of the racetrack. To our happy surprise, the program showed that our own Mr. Howard had an entry in the third race—a claiming race for three year olds, as I recall.

We watched with great interest as preparations for the race began, and the animals were led onto the track. Eventually we caught sight of Howard leading a big, beautiful gray to the starting line, while his jockey sat perched on top.

"And just how much does Mr. Howard owe us these days?" I asked Wilton, as I peered through his binoculars.

"I would have thought you'd know that down to the penny, dear."

"Well, of course I do. I just wondered if you did."

The race was thrilling, at a mile and an eighth. And though Mr. Howard's horse, Sterling, labored to make the distance, he fought off the favorite down the stretch and seemed to have won by a nose. But unfortunately for Mr. Howard, a protest was lodged and upheld, and his beautiful gray was disqualified.

Afterwards, we went looking for Mr. Howard in the stables to express our condolences and, after some searching, found him, in his horse's stall, raging at his jockey.

"You ride like an idiot, you stupid fool."

"I bumped him and got caught. So what?"

"If you've got to foul, foul so nobody can see."

At that, Mr. Howard noticed our presence and turned to greet us, rather surprised.

"You'll have to pardon me, ma'm," he said, all smiles. "The stable is no place for a lady."

"I understand perfectly well, Mr. Howard. Wilton swears like a sailor at home."

"I do not."

"You do to."

Howard laughed and introduced us to his jockey—his cousin, Joe, he told us, from Missouri. This cousin—or so-called—was a lightly built young man, not much over five feet tall who, evidently, had forgotten to shave that morning.

"How do you do, ma'm?" He took my gloved hand, made a show of kissing it, then looked me up and down as if he were appraising a horse he might ride.

"Charmed," I said, pulling away.

"I didn't know you two attended the races," Howard said. "I have an entry in the Nashville Stakes, next Friday. Come out and watch, if you can. We might even win if I can find a jockey who knows his business."

"To hell with you," cousin Joe said.

Howard waved his thumb at him. "These boys don't know what real riding is," he told Wilton.

"I can ride better than you," cousin Joe put in. "You're too old and fat."

Mr. Howard's face went red with anger, but he held his temper.

"Come to the Stakes on Friday, if you can," he told us. "But if you want to see some real riding come on out to my place any Saturday, and I'll show you what an old cavalryman can do."

We told Howard we would try to attend the Stakes, bid him goodbye, and, as we walked away, the shouting match resumed.

"You ride him yourself if you want. It don't mean nothin' to me."

"Maybe I just will."

Moments later, as we strolled down the midway, I asked Wilton if Mr. Howard's hair seemed a bit blacker than it had seemed before.

"His hair? Blacker?" Wilton said.

"Yes. His hair and his beard, too. Blacker, they were, somehow."

We were unable to attend the Nashville Stakes, despite Mr. Howard's invitation, but we learned in the newspapers that his horse, with cousin Joe in the saddle, had, indeed, finished first and won a large purse. After this, I expected Mr. Howard to come into the store to make a payment on account. But after a week rolled past without a sign of him, I insisted that we take him up on his other invitation—that of visiting his farm on some Saturday.

My first impression of the place was that it was rather run down. The fences, which were rotting, were propped up in various places with childlike contrivances of wood, wire and nails. The main house was in definite need of paint and I doubted the roof would stand another winter.

"He hasn't been putting our money into any improvements," I told Wilton. "That's a certainty."

"He's just renting, dear. I don't suppose he has much interest in improving someone else's property."

Mr. Howard welcomed us with open arms. He introduced us to his son, Tim, aged about three—an energetic, if troublesome, boy—and his wife, Josie, a tidy looking woman who never seemed to attend church along with her husband.

"I understand you've been poorly," I said to her. "I hope you're doing better, now."

"Oh, it's just the morning sickness is all. You know how that is."

"Well, if I did, I would certainly not speak of it in public."

Wilton pulled me away, and Mr. Howard reintroduced us to his rude cousin, the jockey who Howard had called Joe at the Fair, but now referred to as Pony.

"I remember," Joe, or Pony, said. "Mr. Pemberton and the little woman."

"She may be," Wilton said, "but you'd better not call her that."

Everyone laughed, except me, needless to say.

Mr. Howard was wearing a pistol on his hip—which gave me cause for apprehension— and, once the introductions were complete, he fetched a second pistol, shoved it into his belt and invited us, along with his crude cousin, to come out back.

"I'll show you what a real rider can do."

He took us to his stable, which seemed much better maintained than the house. He had three fine racehorses there—including the gray he'd raced at the Fair—and he described each of them to us, cataloging the races they'd entered—and won—just like a proud papa.

He went to the tack room and returned with a heavy saddle, but bypassed the thoroughbreds and picked out a sturdy looking mongrel, instead. Once the beast was saddled, Howard showed us out to a little racecourse he'd set up behind the stable, complete with old, straight back chairs for spectators.

He pointed to an old oak tree near the track. "You go stand over there," he told Joe.

Howard mounted the mongrel and took a few turns around the track to heat him up. He seemed quite taken with himself, as he rode, but I wasn't very impressed by his form. He slouched in the saddle and his hands were all wrong.

But on his final lap, Howard turned the horse straight towards us, let out a chilling, rebel yell, and thrust the bridle reins between his teeth. Now—with both hands free and galloping, full tilt—he pulled out his two revolvers, aimed at the oak tree where he had stationed cousin Joe, and began firing with great rapidity.

Joe dove for cover with a scream, but I don't think the rude fellow was in danger for even a moment. Howard shot with uncanny accuracy. Twelve times his guns popped, twelve times a bullet drilled into that tree.

"By God," Wilton exclaimed, swinging his hat in the air. "By God, I haven't seen a sight like that since the war."

Howard, grinning from ear to ear, trotted up to us and slid from the saddle.

"Brilliant," Wilton said. "Absolutely brilliant."

"Words are cheap," Howard said, "but we're going to be having some races later, and I'll know what you really think of my riding by how big your bets are."

"You crazy bastard," cousin Joe yelled, from behind the oak.

Soon after, more guests arrived at the farm, and I recognized a number of them—staunch rebels all. I had expected that and was not disturbed, but then a dozen or so fellows in the loud attire of sporting men arrived with their ladies and, among them, were two of Nashville's most notorious madams.

After the races ended, we left Howard's farm somewhat enriched, but as we rode away in the surrey, I told Wilton it was time we called in our chits.

"Choir boy or no, rebel or no, cavalryman or no, the man can't be trusted, and you've given him an awful lot of our money."

"Money is the only thing you seem to care about," Wilton said. "What about honor? What about right? This man fought for Southern independence for four, long years and was wounded several times."

"We lent him money," I replied. "He promised to pay us back, and when he does, he'll be doing the honorable thing."

"And why is it that I have to do the dirty work? Why do I have to confront him? You're the one who seems the most concerned about it."

"But you're the man, dear. Asking for money is not a job for a woman. Asking for money is a man's job."

The next time Mr. Howard came into the store Wilton demanded payment in full and Howard, quite offended, left the store in a huff. Eventually, we were forced to threaten him with a lawsuit, and this was enough to cause him to send us a check by mail. But the check failed to clear due to insufficient funds, and we took the matter up with our attorney. A court date was set, after many delays, but Mr. Howard failed to put in an appearance, and we were awarded a judgment against him.

Collecting on it proved so difficult that I almost gave up ever seeing the money again, but one day after church, Howard met us on the front steps. He was accompanied by his vile, little jockey—Joe, or Pony, or whatever his name—who tipped his hat and leered.

"It's a pleasure to see you again, ma'm."

Howard pulled a roll of greenbacks out of his pocket and snapped the bills into my husband's hands one by one.

"Here's your damn blood money," he said. "You pretend to be a gentleman, but there are no such things anymore. Everyone betrays everyone for money these days. Hypocrites and Judases is what you all are."

After that we never saw him again and, knowing what I know now, I suppose we were lucky to escape with our lives. I don't doubt that Mr. J. D. Howard wore a shoulder holster under those choir robes of his.

30

Summer 1878
Joe "Pony" Sawyer, Outlaw and Informer
Excerpt from His Confession

Deposition taken by P. D. Haeffy, Police Commissioner, Kansas City, Mo., this twenty-ninth day of March, 1882.

Haeffy: Well, Joe, lets start with your name and particulars.

Sawyer: You know my name.

Haeffy: Yes, but this is a formal statement. Give us your full name, date of birth and so on.

Sawyer: I was born on August 21, 1855 near Keatsville in Clay County. My parents named me Charles Joseph Sawyer Jr., but it got confusing since my father's name was also Charles, so they started calling me Joe.

Haeffy: Very good. We're learning things already. Now, begin at the beginning and leave nothing out.

Sawyer: Should I start with Jess?

Haeffy: Yes, I should say Frank and Jesse are the ones we're interested in.

Sawyer: I first met Jess about ten years ago, before he encumbered himself with a wife. I was eighteen years of age and had just gotten work at Sidney Marion Keats' plantation near Keatsville. I had a job in the stables. I wasn't supposed to know who Jess was, but I've always been clever.

Haeffy: Did General Keats know who he was?

Sawyer: Yes. Frank and Jess would pull off a raid, then hide out at Keats' or other places.

Haeffy: What other places?

Sawyer: I wasn't in with him then, but when I was we'd stay at Keats', Billy Drury's, Jess's mother's, Old Man Rhawn's place in Kentucky, the Ford's in Richmond, and others. I don't want to get anyone in trouble, though.

Haeffy: You're doing just fine, Joe.

Sawyer: Well, I'd always liked handsome horses, and sometimes I'd borrow one without getting the owner's permission, if you know what I mean. I didn't do any harm. I'd just ride them around until they got wore out, then leave them somewhere.

Haeffy: And that's why they call you Pony?

Sawyer: I suppose. I never thought about it.

Haeffy: Would you rather I called you Pony?

Sawyer: Call me what you want.

Haeffy: Go on.

Sawyer: Well, at Keats' I fell in with this colored boy who liked to borrow horses, too, but he got caught. To save his skin he snitched on me. They let him off easy, but I got seven years. I'm only snitching on Jess because he wants to kill me. Whatever comes, he's brought this upon himself.

Haeffy: Let's leave that until later. It's best if we keep things in order.

Sawyer: I went to prison but got pardoned out on good behavior after serving three years, six months and fourteen days. It was March 25, 1877, and, having no other plans, I borrowed another horse—it was black with four white feet—and went over to Keatsville.

Keats had got fat, by then. He might have been a great general once, but now he's only fat. His wife is still very pretty, but she never liked me much.

I asked Keats if I could have my old job back. He said he was breeding mules, now, not race horses, and I never liked mules. But I've always been lucky, and it happened that Jess was visiting at Keats' place when I arrived.

He'd grown a thick beard and dyed it black, but I still recognized him.

"I learned a lot in prison," I told him. "Now I want to learn how to rob banks and trains."

"I'm out of that line of work," Jess said. "But if you're as good with horses as you say you are, you might want to come up to Nashville. I have a string of thoroughbreds and we hold races. I might even take them on the Southern circuit some day."

Haeffy: *You left for Nashville, then?*

Sawyer: *No. Jess had some business to conclude with Keats first. He was borrowing a large sum of money from him but never told me how much. Then Colonel Brown showed up.*

Haeffy: *Colonel Jax Brown, the legislator?*

Sawyer: *Yes. Keats sent a boy to the depot to pick him up, and when he arrived me and Jess were sitting on the porch. Jess introduced us and Brown shook my hand. He didn't have much of a grip unless it was around a bottle of rye. He asked Jess how things had been.*

"Not good," Jess said. "I lost a lot of money in beans."

"Beans?" Brown said. "I thought you were raising horses."

"Yes, but when Hayes got elected I thought there was going to be another war so I speculated in beans."

"You should stay with what you know."

"All I know is robbing trains."

A pretty, little colored girl brought us out some drinks, and there was ice in the glasses. We drunk them and didn't talk for a minute. Then Jess asked Brown if he'd brought him any good news.

Brown shook his head. "I don't believe anything can be arranged at this time."

Keats had come out by then. He had on a suit that was very rich looking, but I thought the lapels stood out too much and made him look like a Hoosier.

"The political situation is very delicate," Keats said.

"I'm willing to surrender," Jess told him, "but only if it is clear that I surrender as a prisoner of war."

"Things are not the same as they once were," Brown said. "Some Democrats are more Union than loyal. Some are more railroad than anything. The thing for you to do is to go back to Nashville and be quiet."

"Frank seems happy enough in Nashville," Keats said.

Jess said, "Frank has no principles anymore."

We left for Nashville the next day. Jess didn't want to ride horseback all that way so we took the train. But he had a sawed-off shotgun, a Winchester rifle, two Colt revolvers, three Smith & Wessons, some extra cartridge belts and a small valise in which he carried more cartridges. He didn't think it wise to carry all these on the cars, so we shipped the Winchester, the Smith & Wessons and the extra cartridge belts to Nashville in a crate. He had me go to town and buy the biggest umbrella I could find and he carried the shotgun concealed in that.

Haeffy: *And what did you do in Nashville?*

Sawyer: *Not much of anything. Jess had horses, like he said, and we ran in some races. We won sometimes, but whatever Jess won he usually lost at poker.*

His wife was named Zee. She wasn't very pretty, and she was too religious for me. Their little boy was named Jesse, too, but they called themselves the Howards, and they were afraid to tell the boy his real name for fear of discovery. They told him his name was Timmy Howard, and I used to pester him about it.

"You sure your name's Timmy?" I'd say. The kid didn't know what I was talking about. "My name ain't really Pony, you know. Maybe yours ain't really Tim."

It was great fun, but Jess didn't like it so I stopped.

Haeffy: *Did you see Frank while you were there?*

Sawyer: *Yes. His wife stayed with us for a while, and she was a pretty one. She'd just had a baby, but she couldn't make milk. Jess's wife had just had twin babies, but they both died, so she took the baby and nursed him herself. Frank didn't come by much because relations between him and Jess were cool. I think it had something to do with Northfield.*

Haeffy: *And just when did Jesse teach you to rob trains?*

Sawyer: *Well, Jess and Zee and me were sitting around in the living room one night. She was reading her Bible, Jess was cleaning his Colts, and I was drinking rye. The kid, Timmy, was playing on the floor, and it was all about dull enough.*

Then Jess said, "Well, Pony-boy, I guess this is as good a time as any to teach you how to rob trains."

I was glad to hear that. I'd worked hard tending his horses and he still hadn't paid me for it.

The kid got real excited. "Can I be the brave engineer, papa?"

"You sure can," Jess laughed.

The kid ran to the bedroom and came back with this set of pull-trains he had. He started running them along the floor making train sounds. This wasn't what I'd expected, but Jess knew his trade so I went along.

"First thing to do," Jess said. "Is build an obstruction across the track. Usually there's rocks or something."

"Here, honey." Zee handed him a couple of spools of thread and some knitting needles. "I imagine you can use these."

"Those'll do just fine, thanks."

"Don't mention it, honey."

Haeffy: *This doesn't seem very important.*

Sawyer: *You told me to leave nothing out.*

Haeffy: *So I did.*

Sawyer: *Right after this, I figured I was getting stale around Nashville so I went back to Missouri. I bumped into Jack Doyle at the Ford's place in Richmond. I'd met him in prison, so I knew he was a good man.*

Charlie Ford was there but not Bob. I told them I was in with Jesse James and asked if they wanted to knock around with me and see what we could rob. Doyle went with me but not Charlie. He was still trying to make a go of it working in his sister's store. Me and Doyle waylaid some travelers in various places.

Haeffy: *Do you remember any particulars?*

Sawyer: *We did all that in Arkansas. The only crimes I ever committed in Missouri are the ones you already agreed to pardon me for.*

Haeffy: *So I thought.*

Sawyer: *After a few months I got a wire from Jess who said that he was getting lonely in Nashville and that he wanted me to come up and keep him company.*

Haeffy: *Pony, we've been at this for over an hour but still haven't touched on anything very interesting.*

Sawyer: *Well, right after this we took a trip to Las Vegas, New Mexico and held a parlay with Billy the Kid.*

Haeffy: *Billy the Kid? The famous outlaw?*

Sawyer: *How many Billy the Kids do you know about?*

Haeffy: *Only one.*

Sawyer: Jess had a lot of debts in Nashville, and he was thinking about emigrating to New Mexico and starting a cattle ranch. So we went down and stayed at some hotel that was owned by an old friend of his from the war.

Haeffy: Do you remember his name?

Sawyer: Jess called him Dickie. His wife was a good cook although not much to look at. The hotel was passable. In Las Vegas they race horses right around the square downtown and I liked that. But it was very hot and dry, and neither of us liked the weather much.

Haeffy: When did you meet Billy the Kid?

Sawyer: It was right after dinner one night. We ate with the other guests. Business men and ranchers, mostly. Jess talked about ranching with them, and it was all boring enough. Nobody knew who we were, but there was this young fellow at the table who seemed pretty rough, and he kept throwing looks in my direction.

Haeffy: Go on.

Sawyer: After dinner, Jess and me sat outside in this courtyard and smoked cigars to get some relief from the heat. That was when this Dickie told Jess that the rough boy at dinner was Billy Bonney, better known as Billy the Kid, and that the Kid wanted to meet him.

"You've been telling people I was here?" Jess said.

"Just him," Dickie said. "If you can't trust Billy the Kid, who can you trust?"

"Some sort of horse thief, ain't he?"

"Haven't you read about him?"

"Mostly I read about me."

After awhile Jess was convinced, and this Dickie told us to go back to our room and he brought in the Kid.

"Billy Bonney," Dickie said. "Shake hands with Jesse James."

Jess held out his hand, and Billy looked at it, then looked at me, then back at Jess.

"That's Jesse James?" He grinned and took Jess's hand. "I didn't think you was so old."

"Well, I am," Jess said.

He asked Dickie to leave so they could talk and, then, he told me to go outside and watch the door. I didn't like his brusque manner much, so I went looking for this señorita who had been making eyes at me.

After I found her, I didn't see Jess until later when I went back to our room.

Haeffy: *What happened then?*

Sawyer: *Jess was lying on the bed, propped up on four or five pillows. He had a big cigar clenched in his teeth and his hands clasped behind his head. He was naked to the waist and there were the scars all over his chest from his old wounds.*

"I thought I told you to guard the door," he said.

"I was guarding it."

"I didn't see you."

"I was staying hidden."

"Go wet a washrag for me."

He had some sort of infection in his eyes and was always sending me for washrags.

"There's a hundred men who'd ride with me if I asked 'em," he said. "A thousand men. I don't need to recruit horse thieves like Billy the so-called Kid. I told him good men were getting hard to find these days, and do you know what he said?"

I told him I didn't.

"He said, 'That's because you got 'em all killed at Northfield.'"

I gave Jess the washrag and he threw it at me. "You were supposed to be watching the goddamn door."

It was always scary when he got like that.

"He told me how he fought in the Lincoln County Wars," Jess said. I told him I'd fought in a real war and for principles, not just cows. I suppose we'll both burn in hell one day, if what the Bible says is true, but at least I'll be burning for my principles. Hell, I never asked to be the greatest outlaw ever."

The next morning we started back for Nashville.

31

October 1879
Mark Talbot, Court Reporter
Kansas City, Missouri

It always pleases city-folk to imagine that a childhood spent on a farm is pristine and ideal. But, in real life, I never found it so. The work was hard and there always seemed to be more of it. As for living close to nature, well, nature seemed scatterbrained to me, even treacherous, and I couldn't wait to be freed from the oppression of it.

I was six years old, in seventy-four, when the 'hoppers first came—millions upon millions of them, blacking the sky and covering the ground. They ate everything in their path, then did it again the next year, and the year after that.

In seventy-nine, when I was eleven, the rain fell and fell and fell. Unceasing, it was, and the mud was everywhere even into summer.

At school, my friends spread tales of cats and small dogs— even babies—falling into the mud and being sucked straight down to the devil. And I could believe it—I'd had my shoes sucked right off my feet by that mud, afterall.

Playing at being Jesse James was our favorite diversion, but it seemed, around this time—during the Wet Year—that the real-life Jameses had disappeared right off the face of the earth. Nothing had been heard of them since the Northfield raid, three years before, and in the schoolyard, some boys began to spread the story that they were dead, killed in the wastes of Minnesota.

My family and I were in church one Sunday when Frank and Jesse—or Jesse, leastways —made his come back. It was late in the year, I know, because the ground was finally dry. We were standing in the pew, singing hymns, and I always sang as loud as I could for singing in church was the only time I was ever allowed to raise my voice.

"'There's a church in the valley by the wildwood...'" I hollered.

Right then, the doors burst open, bang, and Mr. Henry Rusie, editor of the Liberty Picayune, came charging down the main aisle with a bundle of newspapers thrust under his arm.

"The Glendale train has been robbed," he cried. "They've struck the Glendale train."

The singing stopped short and, after a hushed moment, a wave of excitement rolled across the congregation.

"The train robbed?"

"Was it Jesse?"

"Is Jesse back?"

In the clamor and confusion, I sprang to my feet without thinking, only to have my father grab me by the coat-tail and pull me back down.

"Don't make a spectacle of yourself."

He wasn't a wicked man, my father, but the war had done something to him—the war and the 'hoppers and the rain— too damn much for a human being to bear.

"They struck like lightening," Henry Rusie called out. "They beat the messenger senseless and made off with fifty thousand. Read all about it in the Picayune."

People mobbed him and bought newspapers hand over fist. I was just dying for my father to do the same, but he didn't. A pinch-penny, I always took him to be, although I know better, now.

"They disappeared into the night with their booty," Mr. Rusie called. "Read all about it."

I was dying to know more, but we always went straight home after church. As we drove off, I noticed a commotion at the colored church across the way—loud voices and a hubbub. I guessed Henry Rusie was spreading the news there, too, but as fraternizing with coloreds was unthinkable for me, I never found out.

Since all of Sunday, and not just the morning—at least according to my father—was the Lord's day, we sat around the parlor the rest of the afternoon. Me, my mother, my little brother John, and my sisters—Faith and Grace—contemplated and prayed, while my father read aloud from the Bible.

"'Man is born unto trouble as the sparks fly upward.'"

I had two other brothers, but both of them died. Matthew swelled up from the dropsy and died when I was four. Luke had died the day he was born. I had another sister, Hope, the oldest of my siblings, but she had run off with a young man from Kansas City—a sporting man, father said—and after that he never allowed us to speak her name.

"'My days are swifter than a weaver's shuttle.'"

After supper, I went straight to bed, but I couldn't sleep. I awoke early the next morning eager to get to school. I darted to the hen house to collect the eggs, quick as I could, but the rooster, who had always been my adversary, dove on me from the rafters.

He pecked me hard, a half dozen times, right on the top of the head, before I could whack him and get him off me. When I got back to the kitchen, father saw the blood.

"Can't you even collect eggs without getting hurt at it?" he asked. "He's a dilatory boy," he told my mother.

Later, when I arrived at school, the yard was in turmoil. No one worked the tetter-totters, no one played at baseball, all the children just milled around in gyrating, little clumps, talking loud and all at once.

"They captured the station-house and took hostages."

"They destroyed the telegraph and made the agent stop the train."

"They made the engineer break down the door with a coal-sledge."

Then, Olive Hanks—tall and skinny as a beanpole—moved towards us from a tree stump near the schoolhouse door. Poor as dirt, her people were—the kind that the women at church made up food baskets for—and the only white folk the rest of us could look down upon.

We teased Olive without mercy when we could, so she kept to herself. But now, in the hard muck of the schoolyard, she walked right up to a gaggle of her betters, took center stage, and commenced.

"I knew all along Jesse wasn't dead," she crowed. "Heard all about it from my uncle, lives up in Platte. After Northfield, Frank and Jesse rode through up there. Just past Ridgley, close by Dicks Creek. They come to a house where an old widow woman lived..."

I suppose it was the one time in her life that Olive Hanks ever held an audience spellbound. At her wedding, a few years later, people stood at proper attention, I recall. At her funeral, too, some years after that, everyone was silent. But that time in the schoolyard, I think, was the only time anyone ever really paid any mind to Olive Hanks.

"The widow didn't hardly have no food in the house," she went on, "but she gave what she had to Frank and Jesse— biscuits and clabber was all—and, while they ate, Jesse saw there was tears in her eyes."

"Tell us, Mother, why are you crying?"

"Because my little farm is mortgaged to the hilt, and because the payment is due today."

Frank and Jesse, or so Olive's story went, gave that old widow woman the thousand dollars she needed to pay the mortgage, then left and watched from the woods until the banker arrived. Once he'd gotten his payoff, Frank and Jesse rode on out ahead of him, found a covered bridge he'd have to cross, hid inside, waylaid him, and stole the money back.

"They rob the rich," Olive said, "and give it to the poor."

The tale gave Olive quite a bit prestige at school for a time, and she was called upon to retell it at every recess. With each retelling she embellished it some, a little here, a little there — the widow was gray-haired and stoop shouldered, the banker wore a top hat and arrived in a four-horse carriage.

I believed it all without hesitation—there was no reason not to, afterall. But a month or so later, one Sunday after church, when my family was sitting in the parlor, praying, my father, without warning, snapped his Bible shut and chortled. It was all very strange.

"I'm sorry," he said, grinning from ear to ear, "but just this morning at church, Jim Clemens told me the finest story."

He seemed so jolly, the rest of us didn't know what on earth to make of it.

"You see," father began, "after the Glendale robbery, Jesse was riding the back roads over near Shibley's Point, when he came to a little house owned by a widow woman..."

Well, it turned out to be the very same story Olive Hanks had told in the schoolyard, only a little different in its details— this widow's husband had died in the war, while serving with Sidney Marion Keats. She was young and pretty, not old and gray. Frank wasn't with Jesse, in my father's version of the story, and it had all happened in Adair County, not Platte, and after the Glendale robbery, not Northfield.

"She offered to feed them," father continued, "even though she didn't have much on hand—just eggs and coffee. While she fried up the eggs, they noticed she was crying, the tears runnin' down her cheeks like rain-water..."

My mouth hung wide open the whole time—leastways that's what my sister told me later—and when the story was done, my mother dared to speak.

"But surely, you don't condone thievery."

Father just grinned. "But don't you see? They rob the rich and give the money to the poor."

I don't suppose I ever saw him happier and it lasted, oh, for weeks, I should say. But soon the rains started up again and the next year the hoppers came, and when the banker come around to collect our mortgage, there was no Jesse James to pay it. My father always scraped the money together, somehow, and I can remember, even now, sitting with him at the kitchen table every month, doing the figures with a fat pencil while he counted out every cent we had.

"Frank and Jesse," he'd say, and he'd tell the story again, just like Olive Hanks. It was all that kept him going, sometimes.

32
November 1879
THE NEW YORK EMPIRIC

AN ATTEMPT TO KILL JESSE JAMES
— ☆ —
Ev Russell's Claims of Shooting the Bandit-King
Are Finding Doubt in Some Informed Circles

Everett Russell, a detective in the employ of Police Commissioner P. D. Haeffy of Kansas City, claims that he shot and killed Jesse James three days ago near Aberdeen, Missouri.

Russell says that as he rode along with James and his gang, one day, he fell in behind Jesse, pulled his revolver and fired. The bullet struck home, blood gushed from the wound, and James fell from his horse, a dead man.

After the shooting, a running fight ensued between Russell and Jesse's men, and Russell was shot in the leg. Now, he is under guard at the Union Hotel in Kansas City, surrounded by officers and detectives, while he recuperates from his wounds. He lies in bed with revolvers at the ready.

"None of Jesse's friends will catch me napping," he says.

Until last month, Russell had been serving a term in prison for his part in the Otterville train robbery in 1876, but he was pardoned out on the proviso that he aid officers in killing or capturing Jesse James.

In the course of this pursuit, he went to Jesse's mother's home, near Kearney, Missouri, and inquired about the outlaw's whereabouts. Immediately, he was seized from behind, blindfolded, and led into the timber. When his eyes were uncovered, he found himself in Jesse's camp. There, he recognized Joe "Pony" Sawyer and Jack Doyle, both ex-convicts, among the bandit-king's court.

He greeted them, then inquired as to the whereabouts of his old friend, Frank James.

Jesse said, "My brother died of consumption, four years ago, in Poplar Bluff, Arkansas."

Russell rode with the gang for several weeks until Jesse determined they should rob the bank at Aberdeen. When he was able, Russell informed Commissioner Haeffy of the impending raid and Haeffy, with a dozen armed men, arrived in Aberdeen and took up positions in and around the bank. But on the evening before the robbery, Jack Doyle went into town for the purpose of buying whiskey and there Doyle discovered the presence of the police.

"Some son of a bitch betrayed us," he told Jesse when he returned to camp.

Russell feared that suspicion was on him and so determined to kill James at his first opportunity. This presented itself the next morning, as he, James, Sawyer and Doyle were riding down the road.

His story seems plausible enough. Sheriff Naylor has confirmed Russell's employment as a detective, but large bodies of men have been scouring the country for days and have yet to find any trace of Jesse James's body.

Capt. P. P. "Monk" Ferris, of the Pinkerton National Detective Agency, thinks the whole tale is a pack of lies.

"Russell would never have dared pull a stunt like that on a man as dangerous as Jesse James," he says.

"It's more likely that Jesse was in on the whole thing and that it was some sort of plot. My belief is that, for sometime now, Jesse has been attempting to convince us that he is dead in hopes that we will give up our relentless pursuit."

In seeking other opinions in the matter, we sent a correspondent to Stillwater Penitentiary where the Younger Boys are serving life terms for their part in the Northfield, Minnesota, robbery. Both Bob and Jim Younger refused comment, but Cole—who says he is a reformed man—was happy to give his opinion.

"Everett Russell and I were comrades in arms during the late war," Younger said. "He was always loyal, above all else, but I suppose that in the awful desperation that prison fosters, he might have been forced into becoming a detective. Beyond that, I find no contradictions in his story. From what I have read of Jesse James's character, the only sensible way to get at him would be from behind."

Our correspondent then asked Cole if it were true that Jesse had attempted to kill his brother, Jim Younger, after the Northfield robbery.

"Five men participated in the Northfield robbery besides my brothers and I," Cole said. "Three of those were killed, but the two men called Howard and Woods escaped. If there had been any men calling themselves James among us, I would certainly have known about it."

Cole says prison life has been hard on him, but that he now works in the prison hospital and is grateful for the opportunity that the people of Minnesota have given him to reform himself.

33
Summer 1880
Joe "Pony" Sawyer, Outlaw and Informer
Excerpt from His Confession

Deposition taken by P. D. Haeffy, Police Commissioner, Kansas City, Mo., this twenty-ninth day of March, 1882:

Haeffy: You don't remember any dates concerning the murder of Everett Russell?

Sawyer: No. But I remember I was at Billy Drury's when Ev was killed. I hid out in the barn and Billy brought me beans. He'll vouch for me. I never killed anyone. It was Tot and Jess. Not me.

Haeffy: Tot being Tot Rhawn.

Sawyer: Yes. Jess's cousin. Old Man Rhawn's boy. His real name was something else, but everyone called him Tot because he was so big. It was a joke, you see. Like you call a little kid a tot, but Tot, see, he was big.

Haeffy: We understand, Pony. You don't have to explain.

Sawyer: Jess and Tot caught up with Ev in Nebraska somewhere. Jess put a couple of bullets in him, but he was still alive when Jess scalped him. I met them later at Jess's mother's. While we were there, Tot told me all about killing Ev. I think he enjoyed it, especially the scalping part.

Haeffy: And now that Tot Rhawn is also dead, there are no other witnesses to Everett Russell's murder?

Sawyer: Except Jess.

Right after that Jess and I went to Dora Ford's, Bob Ford's sister's. She had a store over by Richmond. At first I thought she was too old for me and too stocky, but she wasn't entirely unpretty.

A few days later Jack Doyle showed up. Him and me and Jess knocked around for awhile to see what we could rob, but there was nothing. After that Doyle and Jess and Tot went to Alabama and robbed the United States paymaster at Muscle Shoals. They got $5,200 and killed the paymaster, but I didn't have anything to do with that either.

Haeffy: *You never killed anyone, did you?*

Sawyer: *No sir. Never.*

Jess got back to Nashville safe, but Doyle got himself captured. He was eating supper in an oyster bar when the officers surrounded him. We read about it in the papers. Doyle got a Pinkerton, but they still captured him.

Jess and I went over to Frank's, and Jess told him that Nashville wasn't safe anymore because Doyle might talk.

"You might as well throw in with me," Jess said.

"You know what I think about that," Frank told him.

"At least you ought to get out of Nashville."

Frank said he supposed Jess was right, and the three of us lit out for Old Man Rhawn's in Kentucky. It was forty miles from Nashville to Blair, but we got there by sunup. Tot wasn't home, but Mary was.

Haeffy: *Mary? That would be Mrs. Rhawn?*

Sawyer: *Yes. Tot's stepmother. Old Man Rhawn's wife. Jess was sweet on her.*

Haeffy: *I thought he loved his wife.*

Sawyer: *Yes, but you know how that is. He gave Mary a gold watch he'd got when he robbed the Mammoth Caves stage. She was young and pretty as a picture. I'll never know why she married Old Man Rhawn.*

Haeffy: *That's not for us to say, Pony.*

Sawyer: *I suppose not.*

Jess's wife, Zee, came about a week later in a wagon with her children and all their possessions. Charlie Ford was driving. She and Mary didn't get on too well.

"Why, I've heard ever so much about you," Zee said.

"Likewise, I'm sure," Mary said, but she wasn't sincere, I don't think.

One day Mary spotted some officers riding up the lane outside the house, and we figured they was after us.

"My God, we'll all be killed," she said.

"Don't you fret, honey," Zee told her. *"Stay around my husband and you'll soon become accustomed to the rough life."*

Zee got Mary and the children down on the floor, and the rest of us went to the windows with our guns.

"I guess you're in with us, now," Jess said to Frank.

"Yes," Frank said, *"I might as well be shot for a sheep as a lamb."*

But the officers must have been after somebody else for they rode right on by, and that very day we entered into an agreement to rob a train—Jess, Charlie Ford, Tot Rhawn, myself and Frank. Charlie and I were very excited about it.

Haeffy: That would be the robbery at Winston?

Sawyer: Yes. But we didn't get around to it right off. Jess first sent Charlie to Kansas City with Zee where she was to rent a house. Frank went away to get his family, but I don't know what he did with them. Jess and I took a train to Kearney and went to his mother's.

Charlie met us there once Zee was safe. Frank arrived about a week after that. Then Tot came, and we laid our plans, but it all went bad.

Jess had a toothache and by the time we got to Winston it had swelled his jaw and face. Then, it started raining, so we decided to give up on the train. We stopped at a house and asked for lodging. The owner was a Dutchman, but I don't remember his name. Jess dosed himself with laudanum and went to bed. The rest of us blacked our boots and ate supper.

In the morning, the Dutchman went to town, and when he came back, we learned from the papers that President Garfield had been shot. A man came up to him in a railroad station and fired two shots. One struck him in the arm, the other in the back. Lived for months before he died.

Haeffy: We know that, Pony. It's common knowledge.

Sawyer: The news cheered Jess some. He was feeling pretty low because of his toothache.

"Was it a Southern man that done it?" he asked.

He was disappointed when he found it wasn't.

Haeffy: *Could we get on with things?*

Sawyer: *Well, we then returned to Jess's mother's, and Jess got his tooth pulled. After a week or two, we decided to make another try at a train. This time we all went separately and met in the woods near the tracks. It was decided that Charlie and I should get on the train at Cameron, and that Frank, Jess, and Tot should get on at Winston. Charlie and I were to capture the engine, while the others got into the passenger cars and robbed the express.*

We left our horses in the woods where we could get them later. It was a long walk to Cameron, and since Charlie and I hadn't had any supper, we went into town early and bought some candy. After that we boarded the train.

The rest of them boarded at Winston, as planned. When Frank gave the signal, Charlie and I made our way to the front of the train, went over the top of the tender, and captured the engineer and fireman. But then something went wrong.

Someone in the cars pulled the emergency cord and the train stopped. I heard gunfire and screaming. Jess yelled at us to get the train moving, but the engineer said he couldn't because of the emergency brakes. Charlie hit him with his pistol and told him he would kill him if he didn't. The engineer threw open the throttle, but Charlie wanted to kill him anyway.

"No Charlie," I said. He had his gun at the man's head, but I pushed it away and stepped between them.

Haeffy: *That was good of you.*

Sawyer: *Yes, it was.*

When the train got back near the place where we'd left the horses, Frank signaled us to shut down the steam, and we all jumped off.

"I think we killed two," Frank said.

"I got a passenger," Jess said.

They were the murderous ones, not me.

34

September 1881
Jesse James
Letter to The Kansas City Loyalist

Indian Territory
Dear Mr. Editor,

> *For sixteen years my enemies have hunted and hounded me and now they have succeeded in driving me into the wilderness. Me & my wife are forced to scratch out a living from soil that is nothing better than dust & rocks. We draw our water from a mile away.*
>
> *My little children cannot stand another winter in these surroundings, but we dare not show our faces in our own native state. We would dearly love to visit my poor mother, crippled by a Pinkerton bomb, as her grandchildren would be a comfort to her. But her house is always watched, and I must move with caution & trust no man. My brother Frank, in the last throws of the illness that took him, dared not even visit a physician.*
>
> *I have taken advantage of these pages many times to offer myself for surrender as a prisoner of war, but no longer does that seem possible.*
>
> *The so-called governor of Missouri is no true Democrat but a tool of the railroads. He deluded the loyal men of the state into voting for him, but now he has shown his true colors by taking money from the railroads & putting it on my head. I attended the Democratic convention last year as a delegate from a place I dare not name and*

tried to warn the people against him, but, alas, I was shouted down by the Chicago men that the governor surrounds himself with.

There used to be democracy in this country and the people once had hope, but democracy exists no longer. The Pinkertons, the railroads & the bankers run all, now, and have set the game so no others can play. To divert the people's attention, they fill their heads with sensational lies and blame Jesse James for all the troubles in the world.

Now I see that Prosecutor Van Gorder has begun assassinating my character in the press. He makes me out to have horns & split feet, but ask my wife & little children if I have such accouterments. I congratulate Prosecutor Van Gorder on sending Jack Doyle to prison. I agree that robbers & killers, such as I understand this Doyle to be, should be punished, but when Van Gorder accuses me of murdering one of his witnesses he goes too far. I do not know this Jack Doyle from Adam, why would I kill a witness against him?

I have been living the life of a fugitive since I was seventeen years old, but I am no longer a boy. I was shot down five times during the war, and all the old lead in my body is beginning to weight me down. All I want from this life is to be allowed to watch my little children grow. I make no demands on the state of Missouri, the legislature, or the Democratic Party, but if Van Gorder & the governor can find it in their hearts to allow me to live in peace, I will never be heard from again.

Sincerely,
Jesse W. James

35

November 1881
Mary Rhawn Sievers, Widow
Logan County, Kentucky

How did you ever find me? You must be disappointed. All the stories say how pretty I was, but, now, I'm wrinkled as a prune.

It's been years since Jesse was murdered, but I remember it perfectly. The whole story is right there, in the quilt that hangs on the wall. I never approved of hanging quilts. They should be useful things, to my way of thinking, not looked at things. But that's what people do, these days—hang quilts from walls. My daughter's the one responsible.

I intended that quilt as a slumber throw for an old sofa I had. I made it with my own hands, and I know each patch. They're remnants from my party dresses. Velvet dresses, they were, and the best velvet, too.

I embroidered the shooting stars with silver gilt and silver thread. They flash with streaks behind them—or that's the idea. Just like Jesse—gone before you can hardly glimpse them. I remember it like it was yesterday—the killings, the betrayal.

It was late autumn. My husband was in Bowling Green for the tobacco auctions. The stalks in the ground were brown and rusty colored. The trees in the orchard were bare and black. The wind had a crack in it. The house had a chill.

Tot and Pony come a-riding in one day after they'd robbed a train, but Jesse wasn't with them. Tot was shiftless—all my stepsons were shiftless. Badness infected the family like measles. Pony wasn't any better.

In the yard, the colored boys had started to slaughter hogs for the winter. In the kitchen, cook and I were boiling water and salting down the meat. When Pony came in, I had salt all over me.

"Afternoon, Mrs. Rhawn." He tipped his hat. "You're lookin' pretty today."

A woman doesn't look pretty when she's up to her elbows in salt, but I smiled at Pony and told him hello.

"Need some help, missus?"

I tried to rub the hair from my eyes with the back of my hand, and ended up with salt all over my forehead. Outside, the hogs were screaming.

"No. I'm fine. I do this all the time."

"Sure now, missus?"

That old slumber throw has gotten very fragile over the years. Pretty soon it'll start coming apart—just like me. Velvet needs to be brushed, you see, and the brushing frays the silk patches and tears them—they're from shirts I made for Jesse. It was a mistake from the start, making that slumber throw from velvet and silk.

My daughter's a much finer quilter than I ever was, truth be known. She gets so fascinated with her stitching that she can't put it down. She's won ribbons and cups at the County Fair. But it never came natural to me. Fact is, I can barely sew a regular stitch.

The first shirt I made for Jesse was a little too snug. He wasn't tall, but, oh, he was a well-built man. Snug under the arms, it was, but he never once complained. Wore it even though it was tight on him and pretended, all the time, that it fit just fine.

"I best keep it here, at your place," he said. "So I can wear it to dances."

He was afraid his wife would see it, needless to say, but it was all innocent. Believe me, it was all so very innocent.

My husband knew about Jesse and me going to dances. He even went with us. He was older and he couldn't dance

179

anymore. I was a lone woman, a widow with a child, and he married me and took us in. I'll always be grateful for that.

Tot went to town one day, and the gossips got hold of him. He came home drunk. It was wash day, and I was helping the colored women with the washtubs in the yard.

"They speak about you in town," Tot said. Big, he was, shiftless.

He followed me into the kitchen. My husband was in Bowling Green. Jesse was with his wife.

Tot said, "I don't like what they're saying."

I told him, "You know they've never approved of me in town. You shouldn't listen to gossip."

"Then you must know what they're saying."

"No. I never get to town. I wish I could get to town, but I never do."

"They say you and Pony are making a fool of my father."

"You know I don't like Pony. Pony likes Dora Ford, and Dora likes him."

"I'm the one who likes Dora."

Pony was in the barn, with the horses. When Tot went looking for him, he left the back door open, and the yard cats come running in. I heard pistols go off and froze. My little daughter started crying in the bedroom and I ran to her. When I looked out the window, I saw Pony ride off as fast as he could—a little boy on a rocking horse.

Tot came back across the yard. The revolver in his hand still smoked. Hunched over, he was, slouched. The back stairs creaked under his feet, he was so big. I was holding my little daughter when he came in.

"I taught the son of a bitch a lesson."

"There's nothing between me and Pony. I don't even like Pony. All Pony cares about is horses."

Tot hit me. "Don't tell lies."

The blue velvet dress I wore to the Midsummer Ball is patched into that old slumber throw. It's colors are the colors of the world at the dance—blue-black nights, white stars and moons, red paper lanterns hung all about.

There was joy in the air, that night, and a string band played "My Dear Old Southern Home." Jesse just loved it. He was so musical. The gossips had a field day.

"Who's that man with Mrs. Rhawn?"

"You wouldn't think she'd flaunt sin so open."

The day after Pony run off, I gave my colored boy a note to carry to a neighbor. We didn't have telephones, in those days, so we sent notes. I don't even remember what was in it, but Tot went after the boy and caught him.

"I got you now," he said when he came back.

He waved the bloody note in my face.

"Tot, what have you done?"

"I killed your little pickaninny, that's what I done. This ain't the first time I caught him carrying love notes. I told him what I'd do if I caught him again."

The whole story is all there, stitched into that slumber throw that hangs on the wall. Pony run from Tot. Tot run from the sheriff.

Now the years fly by, and I've had a stroke. I can't sew anymore. My fingers just don't work right. The doctor listens at my chest and tells me my ticker misses beats. I tell him a heart ain't just a pump, but he just laughs and makes jolly.

36

December 1881
Joe "Pony" Sawyer, Outlaw and Informer
Excerpt from His Confession

Deposition taken by P. D. Haeffy, Police Commissioner, Kansas City, Mo., this twenty-ninth day of March, 1882:

Haeffy: You started having doubts about Jesse after the Blue Cut robbery?

Sawyer: Not exactly. At Aberdeen—where Ev tried to kill Jess — we'd gotten a lot of grief but no money. Then, we only got $103 each at Winston. Frank and Jess killed a couple of men there, and you know how I hate killing. By the time we robbed the train at Blue Cut, I was sick of hearing Jess complain about his teeth and, besides that, we robbed the wrong train again.

Jess thought there was going to be a lot of money on it, but there wasn't. I only got $160 and a brass watch for all my trouble. Charlie Ford found a basket of cake and a bottle of wine in one of the sleepers. Then, when we were about to beat it, Jess tipped the engineer two dollars.

"You've been a bully boy, so drink to the health of Jesse James tomorrow."

' It was very peculiar.

After the divide, I headed for Mary Rhawn's and Tot showed up two days later. He and I got into a shooting scrape in the barn. I snapped a couple of caps at him, and he ran. After that I couldn't see staying around there any longer, so I went down to Dora Ford's.

Haeffy: What did you and Tot fight over?

Sawyer: I'd rather not say.

Haeffy: You have to, Joe.

Sawyer: A woman.

Haeffy: What woman?

Sawyer: I won't say.

Haeffy: All right, Pony. I don't suppose it matters.

Sawyer: A few days later, Tot came after me at Dora's. When I came down for breakfast one morning, there he was, sitting at the table drinking coffee. Dora was at the stove.

"Hello, Pony," he said. I could tell he was looking for trouble.

"I don't speak with liars," I told him and, with that, Tot jumped up and drew his pistol.

"Oh, my God, not in the kitchen," Dora cried.

But it was too late. We fired at about the same time. He shot me through the right leg between the knee and hip, and I shot him through the right arm.

Bob Ford heard the shots, I guess, and ran in. He pulled a revolver, quick as lightening and killed Tot with it.

Haeffy: Bob Ford killed Tot Rhawn, not you?

Sawyer: Yes. I never killed anyone. He even bragged about it later.

"It was a hard shot, but I had to protect my sister."

We carried Tot upstairs. He was groaning and crying, but he only lived about five minutes. Bob's bullet went fair through his head. Dora had a devil of a time getting his blood and hair off the kitchen floor. Bob and Charlie buried him that night in the timber, about a half mile away. I couldn't help because of my leg.

Haeffy: He was killed in the morning and died immediately, but you didn't bury him until night?

Sawyer: Yes. Dora had visitors coming and we were afraid they'd see us if we tried to drag the body out. When they came, we made a day of it playing cards. I won $4.37. While we were playing, Dora got scared that Tot might start to stink, but I told her not to worry. It was December and cold and I'd left the windows open.

Haeffy: Who were these visitors?

Sawyer: I don't recall their names. One of them was fat. After they left, Bob and Charlie buried Tot, then we all sat around in the kitchen.

"Jesse will be after you, now," Bob said.

"It wasn't me who killed Tot," I told him. "It was you."

"Do you think Jesse will stop to ask? You saw what he did to Ev Russell."

Jess took hold of Ev's hair with his left hand and put a knife to his scalp. First he'd cut a little, and then he'd pull a little. It didn't take long because Jesse was good at it. He said it was the fate of all traitors.

Haeffy: You saw that, did you?

Sawyer: No, I only heard about it from Tot. I never had anything to do with killing anybody.

Haeffy: Of course not.

Sawyer: Bob said, "You'd better throw in with us, if you don't want Jesse after you."

I asked him why I'd ever want to throw in with him, and he said because he was a detective.

"I don't believe it," I said. "If you're a detective what have you been doing robbing stages and why has Charlie been robbing trains?"

"We're special detectives employed by the governor. He wants to get Jesse and doesn't care how."

Haeffy: Did they tell you exactly when they began working for the governor?

Sawyer: No. But Bob said he could arrange for my surrender and, that if I agreed to testify against Jesse, he'd get the governor to pardon me. I'd been thinking about going straight ever since Blue Cut, but I told him I wanted to think it over more.

The next day Bob and Charlie left. I don't know where they went, but they didn't come back for two weeks. Jess showed up two days after they left.

"What's happened to your leg?" he asked.

It got shot when I fought with Tot, of course, but I didn't want to tell Jess that, so I said I'd got it stealing horses. Dora backed me up. I would have made her pay if she hadn't.

Jess wanted me to go with him to Nebraska to scout out banks, but I didn't want to take any chances. It would have been easy for him to kill me somewhere on the road. I told him I didn't think I could go because of my leg.

"Do you know where Bob and Charlie are?" he said.

I told him I didn't.

"I don't like going alone," he said, but he went anyway.

A week later, detectives raided Dora's, but I was in town so they didn't get me. Bob and Charlie came back two days after that.

"The law's on to you now," Bob said, "and it won't be long before Jesse is, too. If you want to save yourself, you'd better throw in with us."

I figured he was right so I said I'd surrender if it could be arranged to my satisfaction. I told him I wanted it all kept secret until Jess was either killed or captured, because there were sneaks and traitors all over the place.

Bob and Charlie didn't want to risk seeing the governor again, so they had Dora do it. She dressed all in black and wore black veils so she wouldn't be recognized. She arranged it all, and I surrendered to Sheriff Naylor on January 3, 1882.

And that's all I know. I never killed anybody.

37
March 1882
Billy Drury, Farmer
Clay County, Missouri

The last time I saw Jesse James alive was about a month before Bob Ford did him in. I was to home, like always, and it was raining outside—chilly but not cold. As was my usual practice, I was lazing around in bed, trying to get up the courage to rise and face the dawn.

Then, I smelled coffee. Then, I heard a crash.

"Mornin', Jess," I said, as I stuck my head through the door.

"You got a mop, Billy?" The kitchen floor was awash with brownish water and coffee grounds.

"Why yes, I got a mop. I should say I got a mop. I don't suppose there's a farmer in the world ain't got a mop."

"Didn't mean to wake you," Jess said. "Got here round midnight so I just let myself in."

"That was real thoughtful of you, Jess."

He'd let himself in by breaking a window latch, which, counting the coffee grounds, meant he'd left me with two messes to clean up.

"Looks like you've put on a couple pounds," I said, as I mopped the floor.

"Me?" he laughed. "Billy, I wish I had time to put on weight. Always on the move, you know. Keeps me fit. Teeth been botherin' me, though. Been ramblin' around up in Nebraska. Lots of nice banks up there, but they all got time locks on the vaults."

"Time locks?" I said.

"Yes," Jess said. "They're on the order of locks hooked up to alarm clocks. Why, if you go into a bank to make a big withdrawal, you can't get the vault open unless its a certain time."

"Why that's something, ain't it?" I said. "You know..." I leaned on the mop to rest. "Just a year or so ago, some fellow come round and wanted to put up a shoe factory."

"A shoe factory? Here? Why, don't that just beat it."

He shook his head. "I went down to New Orleans last month to witness that so-called championship fight. Lasted all of ten minutes with Ryan going down at any excuse. And a pretty penny those tickets cost me, let me tell you."

"Damn," I said. "What kind of fight lasts but ten minutes?"

"Damned if I know."

I told Jess I was looking forward to jawing with him some more, but first I had the morning chores to do.

"You just go on and do 'em, Billy, and don't mind me. I got some readin' to catch up on."

"Readin'?" I said. Jess had never been much for that, in my experience.

Then he picked up this book he had, showed it to me, and that explained it all. A dime novel, it was. "Jesse James and the Incredible Steam Posse," it was called.

"Of course," he said. "If you need some help with those chores..."

"No, no, Jess," I said, thinking of the coffee incident. "I suppose I can do them myself."

An hour or so later, when I got back inside, dripping wet from rain and perspiration, Jess was laughing his innards out over the more ridiculous parts of this dime novel. Supposedly, it was an excerpt from the diary of Jimmy Ready, boy inventor.

This Ready boy, according to the story, had built a posse made up of mechanical men and horses driven by steam, with which he pursued the James Boys from Mexico to Canada and back, never quite catching them but coming oh-so-close.

"We've never been pursued by mechanical men, Billy, but, by Lord, it sometimes feels like it."

"I imagine it does."

"I bet they don't write books this good about Billy the so-called Kid."

"I imagine they don't."

"You ain't seen Pony around lately, have you?"

"No, can't say that I have."

"Or my cousin?"

"No, ain't seen Tot either."

Jess shook his head. "Cole and me, we had our troubles, but if there was banks to be robbed or trains to be wrecked, you could count on Cole. Know what I mean?"

"I do," I said.

"Don't know what the world's coming to, Billy. Why, Frank spent half his life tellin' me why we had to fight for the South, and now he says he was all wrong about it. Now, he says we're just common killers. I never harmed a working man, a Southerner, or a woman in all my life, Billy, and I've always tried to do the right thing. God knows that."

"I'm sure He does, Jess."

"Sometimes I think I'll just pack it all in and go somewhere... California, maybe, like my daddy. I got these brochures from this company that sets up emigrants in California for hardly nothing. Cattle, corn, wheat... You can grow anything you want in California. You want to see 'em, Billy?"

I said I did even though I'd seen hundreds of such things myself. California was getting to be all the rage once again—a regular Eden, folks said it was.

Jess got the brochures from his overcoat, spread them on the table, and we talked about what towns sounded best. They were all sunny and warm—or so the brochures said—sunshine all year round in California, it seemed.

"Only trouble," Jess said, "is that the railroads have a pretty tight grip on things out there."

I shook my head. "I suppose you'd do best to stay far away from railroads."

"I suppose."

We looked through these brochures a while longer, then Jess allowed as how he ought to be getting back on the road.

"Be seeing you, pard'," he said, as he swung up into the saddle.

"Be seeing you, Jess," I replied. "Give my best wishes to Zee and the children."

"I'll do that, Billy. And I left two dollars on the table," he said, "to pay for that window latch."

"Thanks, Jess."

He gave his horse a git-up and that was the last I ever saw of my good friend and neighbor, Jesse Woodson James.

A month later, Bobby Ford betrayed him for five thousand pieces of silver—that's what the common wisdom holds, at any rate. But me, I figure Bob just got in a little beyond his depth. You know how it is, you steal a horse, rob a stage or two, and before you know it you've killed Jesse's favorite cousin, and you're forced to turn spy and assassin to get yourself out of the mess. Gun duels at twenty paces are all well and good on the popular stage and in the novels, but in real life, back shooting is all the more practical.

George Jansen

GHOSTS

George Jansen

38
April 1882
THE NEW YORK EMPIRIC

JESSE JAMES SHOT AND KILLED
— ✫ —
The Famous Outlaw Assassinated By a Detective Using a Gun Jesse had Given Him

This morning, in St. Joseph, Missouri, Jesse Woodson James, the notorious bandit and train robber, was shot and killed by Charles and Robert Ford, special detectives in the employ of the governor and the chief of police.

Once the news began to circulate, crowds of people rushed to the little white house on Lafayette St. where the shooting occurred. At first, no one could believe that Jesse was dead, but when this was proven beyond doubt, the officers present had to fight back the mob to keep the house from being stripped for souvenirs.

Statements ascertained from Jesse's wife and the Ford brothers indicate that the James family moved to St. Joseph in December of last year. The Fords, who were pretending to be members of his outlaw gang, began staying with them two weeks ago.

This morning, Jesse sent Robert Ford to buy the morning newspapers, as was his habit. But when Robert obtained them, he noticed a news item concerning an event that was supposed to have been kept secret. He tried to hide this paper from Jesse, but Jesse found it and at breakfast, as he drank coffee and ate toast with marmalade, he discovered the article in question.

"Ho, what's this?" he exclaimed. "It says here that Pony Sawyer surrendered to the authorities two months ago."

He put the paper down and looked the Ford Boys dead in the eyes. "Pony was staying with you and your sister about then, wasn't he?" As he glowered at the Fords, they tried to shrug it off.

"I don't know anything about it," Charles said.

Robert shook his head. "We don't see Dora much."

Then, Jesse's demeanor changed in a curious way.

"Well, that's all right," he said. "If you don't know anything, you don't know anything."

It would have been logical for Jesse to attack the Fords upon learning the news of Sawyer's surrender, and it can only be supposed that he failed to do so because he did not wish to commit murder in front of his wife and children. But the Fords realized he would kill them when he could and, from that moment on, they knew they would have to kill Jesse James in order to save themselves.

After breakfast, Jesse and Charles went to the stable to curry their horses and afterwards returned to the room where Robert waited.

"It's awfully warm in here," Jesse said. He pulled off his coat and vest and laid them on the bed.

"I guess I better take off my pistols, too," he said, "otherwise somebody might see them if I walk in the yard."

Incredulous, Robert Ford watched as Jesse, still attempting to throw off all suspicion, unbuckled his heavy gun-belt and laid his revolvers on the bed by his coat and vest.

Jesse picked up a dusting brush. "Those pictures look awfully dusty to me." In order to get at a picture on the wall, he stepped onto a chair and presented his back to the brothers.

In silence, the Fords crept between the outlaw and his revolvers. Then, at a signal from Charlie, Robert drew his gun—a Smith & Wesson .45 that Jesse had given him not two nights before.

Robert pointed the long weapon at Jesse, not four feet from the back of his head. He cocked it. Jesse turned his head, but too late. Ford pulled the trigger. The muzzle flashed. A well-directed ball crashed into the outlaw's skull and Jesse James fell backwards onto the carpeted floor.

As blood gushed from the wound, a little mongrel dog that Jesse had given his children a few weeks before, dashed into the room and circled around the body, barking at the Fords as if to protect its master from their awful treachery.

Jesse's wife rushed in from the kitchen.

"My God. Robert Ford. What have you done?"

She ran to the side of her husband, knelt, and lifted up his head. Nestled like a baby in his wife's loving arms, Jesse James, the great outlaw, looked up towards heaven, rolled his eyes, and breathed his last.

39

April 1882
Billy Drury, Farmer
Clay County, Missouri

Normally, I shy away from funerals—they remind me too much of that one I'll be forced to attend one day. But I don't suppose I could pass up Jesse's. I'd attended his baptismal, after all. I'd seen him check in, so I couldn't very well miss seeing him check out. And Jess went in style, I must say.

The railroads—those same ones he'd robbed—supplied a special train that brought his body from St. Jo to Kearney. His wife, his mother, and his children—not to mention a dozen special police—rode with the coffin. All along the right of way folks lined up to wave and say goodbye. Little children laid pennies along the tracks for the iron wheels to flatten and kept 'em as souvenirs.

When they unloaded the coffin at the station, a fellow in rebel gray came up to me.

"We're taking up a collection for his widow and orphans," he said, thrusting a cigar box under my nose.

I was tempted to ask if anyone had taken up a collection for all the widows and orphans Jess had made, but I didn't. No sir, I dug through my pockets and gave what I had.

Once the coffin was off the train, six more fellows in gray carried it over to the hotel. They opened it up and long lines of mourners passed by for hours on end. Trains that were supposed to pass straight through stopped at the depot, instead, so the passengers could troop over to Kearney House and take a gander at Jesse James lying in state.

Whilst standing in line, I found myself right behind Roy Ross, proprietor of The Little Dixie Barbershop down in Liberty.

"Terrible tragedy," Roy said, shaking his head. He was a clean, sweet-smelling fellow, as you might imagine—the son of a die hard rebel and the father of one in the making.

"Is it really Jesse, papa?" little Roy said.

Roy sucked in his gut and wiped a tear from his eye.

"No son, it ain't Jesse at all. It's just a fellow who looks like him." He turned to me. "Charlie Ford told the whole story to Press Crumling's cousin, and Press told it to me. Jesse's idea, it was, to fake his death and get the reward money."

"But what about his wife and children?" I said, as three more of those gray clad rebels escorted them from the hotel to a coach.

"Oh, they're in on it, too," Roy said. "Oh, yes. They've been in on it from the start. It's an act they're putting on, just an act."

Zee was crying and the children were, too. Roy was a good man with the shears, but it seemed to me it was him who'd got clipped this time.

Still, when I got to the coffin, I looked Jess over a little more careful than I might have, otherwise, and it was him all right—a bit pudgier in death than he had been in life, somehow, and older looking. But death and morticians always do have a curious effect on a man's appearance.

Once we'd all had a last look, the pall bearers carried Jess down to the church—one his father had founded forty years before, the same one where Jess had accepted the Lord, himself, right after the war.

Those of us that could fit, filed in, and that was when I first laid eyes on Mary Rhawn—the beautiful one, the young and pretty one, the one who was, perhaps, Jesse James' lover.

Unescorted she was, for her husband had left her sometime before.

"You think she'd have some respect," the ladies at the funeral whispered.

"The nerve of her, wearing black."

"Yes, the nerve."

I suppose the ladies would have taken her on even worse if she'd been wearing blue or white or scarlet, for that matter, but that's what gossip is, I suppose.

"Death comes like a thief in the night," the preacher bellowed. "Be ye always ready to meet your Maker."

That was when Jesse's ma went completely to pieces— broke down, and wept like a baby.

"Poor woman," the ladies whispered.

"Damn them Yankees," the menfolk cursed.

Mary Rhawn didn't cry or say a word, just sat and watched.

After the service was over, we made our way out to the farm. Family and friends were the only ones allowed on the grounds. Two black men with shovels stood by the open grave. Eight feet deep, it was, not just six—to discourage grave robbers, or so the story went. When the box was manhandled in, Jesse's ma broke down again.

"Oh God, oh God!" she sobbed. If it was just an act, like Roy the barber claimed, she was sure good at it.

Aunt Loretta, the James's cook, brought out some coffee.

"Can't let folks go away thirsty," she said to me. "Can't have thirsty people running around, even if it is a funeral."

I took a cup, thanked her, drank it straight down, then got into line for another. I never seen so many lines as I did that day—and that was when the general, Sidney Marion Keats, walked over to where I was. A bit portly, he seemed now, but all decked out in a fine looking suit. A gaunt looking fellow I did not recognize was with him.

"Terrible tragedy," the general said, shaking my hand. "Absolutely terrible."

"Yes," I replied. "A dark day for the South."

I was up to the head of the line by that time. I held out my cup to Loretta, and Loretta poured.

"General," she said, "how 'bout you? Colonel Brown, you want some more?"

You could have knocked me over with a stick. I never imagined that the gaunt fellow dragging along behind Sid Keats, was the famous rebel, J. A. X. Brown. His face was drawn and lined. His hands betrayed a tremble. Pale, he was, like he'd been hitting the bottle, hard.

General Keats introduced us.

"Terrible tragedy, terrible." I shook my head. "The South has lost its bravest and best."

Jax Brown looked at me, then right through me.

"Jesse used to stay with you on occasion, didn't he? I remember him saying your name."

"Yes sir," I said. "My house was Jesse's house, you know. Two peas in a pod, that's what we were."

"You're from Clay," Jax Brown said. "You're a farmer, but not a good one, if I recall. You never declared yourself during the war."

"I wouldn't say that exactly."

"I know all about you, Mr. Drury," Brown said. "Jesse rather enjoyed you, but I find that I do not."

He frightened the death out of me—this pale as death fellow—and I snuck off as quick as I could.

"It sure is a good one they're puttin' on today," Loretta said. I was watching from the kitchen window, by this time, while Loretta brewed up more coffee.

"I've seen it all," she said. "Pinkertons, outlaws... a damned hand grenade got thrown right through that very window. But Mr. Frank James is the most peculiar, if you ask me. You know what he said to me, this morning?"

"Frank's here?" I said.

"No, he run out earlier, before the crowds came. You want some more coffee? We got gallons of it. Got white cake too, for later on. Die hard rebels only."

"I don't think I'll stick it out that long."

"You want some for home? I could wrap it up."

"Why, I wouldn't mind a taste," I said, always having been partial to cake. "What was it Frank said to you?"

"Well," Loretta said, "I said to Mr. Frank, 'Thank God Mr. Jesse was baptized proper.' And Frank said, 'Baptism does the most good when taken with soap.'"

Loretta laughed. "Now ain't that a devil of a thing to say at your own brother's funeral?"

The departures were going on around then. The principles—Jesse's wife, still looking brave, and his ma, still weeping, with Sid Keats and Jax Brown on the flanks—had formed a skirmish line alongside the main house. The guests were trooping by, shaking their hands, and shedding a few last tears.

Now, as I ponder the experience from the vantage point of the passing years, it strikes me that the funeral was just a little too legendary. Even the manner of Jesse's death was perfect—being shot in the back by a false friend was as good an act as Crockett falling at the Alamo or Custer going down at the Little Big Horn. And why on earth would a hardened fugitive like Jesse James turn his back on a smarmy, little creep like Bob Ford?

But, no matter how peculiar some of it might have seemed, and no matter what the barbers and gossips say, it was Jesse who got laid to rest, not some impostor. I drank his coffee and ate his cake. I saw his coffin put in a grave that was eight feet deep, not just six. It was locked up tight, and those black men threw dirt upon it. Make no mistake, it was Jesse James who got buried that day.

40

Spring 1882
Whit Smith, Actor, Juggler, and Clown
Chicago, Illinois

In 1882 my wife and I toured the Midwest little suspecting we were about to become supporting players in a real-life tragedy. We were with a good sized show, running continuous varieties from eleven a.m. to eleven p.m. A dozen railroad cars were required to carry the scenery and costumes, and we steamed into Kansas City in late April.

Mr. Milton LeGrow, our producer, could smell a good act fifty miles away. He was sitting in the empty seats of the Theater Tragedian, I recall, supervising the unpacking and smoking a cigar. He was reading a newspaper article about the death of Jesse James, when he suddenly jumped up and dashed out.

He disappeared for a week and didn't return until he'd brought his quarry to earth—that infamous American Judas, Robert Ford, and his less accomplished brother, Charlie.

Within a few days, a melodrama called "The Detective's Vow" was concocted by Bob and Mr. LeGrow. It was a poor little skit, wherein the Fords were to portray themselves, and I was recruited to play Jesse James. Lucy Conatser, the prettiest girl in the show, was cast as Jesse's wife.

Mr. LeGrow had tried to get the real Mrs. James to act in his little play—as she was in need of money—but she'd thrown him out of her house without ceremony.

Mr. LeGrow had school-boys passing out flyers advertising the Ford's theatrical debut almost immediately, and we only had time to rehearse the thing once. On the morning the Fords arrived for that rehearsal the excitement was contagious. Everyone wanted to get a look at the notorious assassins, and as they walked through the doors every singer, hoofer, and thespian in the show dropped whatever they were doing to stare and whisper.

"I thought they'd be taller."

"They'll be dead in a week."

"Why, they're just boys," my wife said. "I'll bet they're frightened out of their wits. You go and make them feel at home, dear."

Well, I'm not a hen-pecked man, but I went up to the boys straightaway and introduced myself.

"Since we'll be working together," I said, "why don't I show you around the theater. Maybe I could give you some tips on acting."

"What do you think, Charlie?"

"Can't hurt, Bob."

I took them backstage and introduced them around. Most of my peers gave them a nod, then quickly retreated. But, as they shook hands, Lucy, the girl who was to play Mrs. James, seemed quite taken with Bob.

"Don't believe all that talk about me," Bob said.

"Why, Mr. Ford. Your hands are freezing cold."

When the rehearsal began, the entire cast and crew turned out to watch, meaning that the first five or six rows of the auditorium were occupied by some of the harshest critics in existence. Bob never betrayed the slightest tremble, but Charlie was as nervous as a pregnant nun.

What happened next wasn't his fault so much as mine. I'd given them both a number of tips, but the one that made the greatest impression on Charlie seemed to be the notion of using his "upstage hand"—that is, the hand that is away from the audience. And it was Charlie's upstage hand that proved his downfall.

On stage, a set depicting the interior of the so-called death house in St. Jo had been thrown up. The front door was stage-right—to the audience's left, that is—and it was through that door that Charlie made his grand entrance. I was sitting in an easy chair, stage-left, and as Jesse James was characterized as a heinous villain in "The Detective's Vow," I was busy ripping the pages out of a Bible. Charlie walked over to me, with his right shoulder to the audience, and read his first line passably well.

"Howdy Jesse, I'm Charlie Ford."

"Will you join a devil's pact to rob and kill?" I asked.

"To the death," Charlie said.

I reached out to shake his hand, just as the script required. Charlie reached for my hand, just as he was supposed to, but unfortunately, he did so with his upstage hand, and his upstage hand was his left.

We stood there for a moment, our mismatched hands dangling in space. Cast and crew burst into gales of laughter, and our young assassin was forever ruined as an actor.

We debuted our play that very afternoon, and the Theater Tragedian was packed—Standing Room Only. Charlie did his best, Bob never quailed, and the audience loved every minute of it.

My wife was doing bird calls in this particular show—they were one of her specialties—and Mr. LeGrow had her come on right after "The Detective's Vow."

"The cry of the red-breasted tit-willow," she announced. "Tweet-tweet. Tweet-tweet."

But that afternoon, not a soul in the audience ever had the joy of hearing the charming cry of that feathered beast—or any of my wife's other bird impressions, for that matter—because every man, woman, and child in the theater was still busy hooting Bob and Charlie.

That's how it went every time "The Detective's Vow" was performed—eight times a day. The moment Bob and Charlie appeared on stage the avalanche of boos and hisses began and didn't stop until my wife finished her bird calls

A few weeks later, after the last show of the evening, I decided to take a walk through the city. It was a warm night, and Kansas City had grown by leaps and bounds since my last visit. I wanted to see the sights, cool off, and relax a bit. I asked my wife to accompany me, but she was worn out.

"If you're not home by two," she informed me. "I'll give you up for dead."

It was well past one when I headed back to the hotel, but I still felt rather wound up—performing "The Detective's Vow" was always a bit unnerving. Then, across from our hotel, who should I see but Bob Ford, slipping into a little saloon of that rather low type that offers a free lunch with every beer sold.

A good snack seemed like just the ticket to inspire sleep in me, but, not wanting to give Bob the impression that I was following him, I walked once more around the block before I entered.

Inside, it smelled of stale beer. The place was almost empty. Bob sat alone at a table in a corner where the walls could protect his back. Instead of going straight up to him, I went to the bar, purchased a beverage and cut myself some bread and cheese. I turned, as if looking for a place to sit and, then, made a show of seeing Bob and going over to join him.

"Hello, Bob."

"Mr. Smith."

He had a beer and an empty shot glass in front of him. His coat was unbuttoned and hung half open. Inside, I could see that he wore a shoulder holster that held a revolver of some sort—I've never been much for guns.

"I'm sorry for this," he said. He closed up his coat then looked left and right. "My life wouldn't be worth a nickel if I went unarmed."

"Do you really think Frank James is out to get you?" I said. The rumors were rampant.

Bob shrugged. "There's always lunatics."

I shook my head and peeled a hard boiled egg. "It hardly seems fair for people to condemn you for what you did."

"You don't know the half of it." Bob laughed—a cynical, disgusted, little laugh.

"If there's one thing I've learned in all my years on the stage," I told him, "it's that there's nothing more fickle than the American public. They'll forget all about you the moment a new sensation comes along. Believe me."

"I hope not," Bob said. "I can make a pile of out of this show business if I play it right."

He then began to narrate his life story for me and I realized, as he did, that he was just the slightest bit drunk.

His tale was almost pitifully naive, something along the lines of a Horatio Alger story. He viewed himself as a self-made man. He'd begun life as the son of a poor, tenant farmer. He'd slaved away in his sister's store. But then he'd made a bold choice, and now he was living in the best hotels, eating in the best restaurants, and money was spilling out of his pockets.

"But if you think I ever got much of that reward money, then you're a fool."

I was incredulous. "You mean to tell me you were cheated by the authorities?"

"I mean to tell you I never got all I was promised. I'll leave it at that."

The Bible contains two different versions of Judas's death, by the way. In Matthew he gives his thirty pieces of silver back to the priests, then hangs himself. In Acts he buys a field with his blood money then falls head long into it, "bursts asunder," and his bowels come gushing out.

A month later, Bob and Lucy Conatser announced their engagement.

"You ought to do something," my wife said.

"I've washed my hands of it," I replied. "The more we talk to Lucy, the more we drive her into his arms."

"Well, talk to Bob then. Have beer with him."

We were in Jeff City, by that time, but, beyond that, the scene wasn't much different. I sat with Bob in a cheap saloon. His back was to the wall. His coat bulged from the shoulder holster he wore.

"You know, Bob, I wonder if it's wise of you to contemplate marriage at this point in your life."

"I don't see how it's your business."

"Well," I admitted, "I've always had something of a crush on Lucy. I suppose half the men in the show do. I'd just hate to see so pretty a girl embark on a life that could end in tragedy."

"Take everything you've heard with a grain of salt," he said. "Lucy's no fool, and I've told her everything. I can protect myself from lunatics and strangers. People get murdered by friends, not strangers, and you can believe me, neither Frank James nor anyone from the gang is out to get me."

I've never quite understood what he was getting at, but that was what he told me.

"I've been doing some thinking," he continued, "and I've got a proposition for you. Producers are the only ones who make any real money in show business."

"Yes," I said. "Its hardly an artist's world."

"I'm going to start my own show, Mr. Smith, and I need a man with experience."

Bob then made a proposition. He wanted me not only to act in his new show—an expanded version of "The Detective's Vow"—but also manage things. In return I would receive a twenty percent interest.

It was a tempting offer. My wife and I never made much more than a bare living as journeymen actors, but I'd already begun seeing assassins everywhere. Whenever we performed "The Detective's Vow" I found myself trying to peer through the footlights—just like Charlie—looking for any killers that might be lurking.

By the time we got to Council Bluffs, I was blundering about the stage like a bull in a china shop, fumbling with my props, and forgetting my lines. Fortunately, the audience was always too busy hooting to notice.

When Bob, Charlie, and Lucy finally took off to start their own show, my wife and I weren't with them. But the day before they left, Bob and Lucy tied the knot. It was quite a wedding. Lucy was about as beautiful a bride as ever existed— wispy, strawberry-blonde hair, transparent blue eyes, a white gown. Every member of the cast, including those who'd shunned Bob like a leper, were there and the church was packed with reporters and curiosity seekers.

Charlie dropped the ring, if I recall.

"What do you think?" I said to my wife, as we watched them drive off into the sunset, in their cozy, little buggy.

"Well," she replied, "at least we won't have to watch the final curtain."

Then, those words from Acts came back to me.

"'...falling headlong, he burst asunder in the midst, and all his bowels gushed out...'"

"Sounds like a shotgun wound," my wife said.

"It does indeed," I replied.

41
Summer 1882
Marion D. Woods, Commercial Fisherman
Seattle, Washington

I had the misfortune to be born into a good Christian family—if there is such a thing. It was all my grandfather's fault. He started out well enough—a full-blooded Crow and a heathen savage. But then some Bible beater got a head-lock on him and convinced him that he was doomed to the fires of hell because Adam and Eve ate an apple back at the beginning of time.

Grandfather started wearing white men's clothes and living indoors. He converted to Christianity and was baptized Joseph White. His Indian friends renamed him, too—White Man Runs His Life, they called him. Worse, still, he joined the Indian Police and, after arresting and persecuting a sufficient number of his brethren, was advanced to the rank of corporal.

He was stationed at Fort Browning on the Blackfoot reservation in Montana, and it was there that he met my grandmother. Woman Who Breeds Horses, her name was and she, being under my his sway, was converted and baptized, too.

Pretty soon, my mother was born. They named her Sarah White and brought her up a Christian. I've never believed the tale of my father's origins but, if Jesus Christ was his own grandpa—or whatever the Trinity makes Him out to be—then I suppose its not impossible that my father was who he claimed he was.

Jesse James was not killed in St. Joseph, Missouri, in 1882, at least according to the tale my family tells. That famous murder was all a fake, they say, because Jesse James really came to Montana in June of that same year, calling himself Dave Woods.

My grandfather had been out of the Indian Police for some time by then, having been wounded in the Nez Perce campaign. The family was living on a ranch near Dillon and the story is that my father—Jesse James, Dave Woods, or whoever he was—first saw my mother when she was riding horseback not far from the ranch.

Tall and bronze-skinned, she was, raven-haired and raven-eyed. The instant my father saw her, he lost his heart forever—well, almost forever, as I'll soon relate. He chased after her, but she'd been born in the saddle, and it took him a lot of hard riding to catch up. When he did, he told her he had never seen a woman so beautiful.

"I'd very much like to come calling," he said.

"Are you a Christian man?" my mother said.

"My father was a Baptist minister."

"But are you a Christian man?"

My father shook his head. "I was baptized long ago, but I've been wandering the wilderness ever since."

They went directly to a church—I find that hard to believe, myself—and when they got there, it happened there was a prayer meeting going on. The people were down on their knees and the preacher told my father to get down on his knees, too.

Father was an obstinate man and never liked doing what he was told, but, still, everyone else was on their knees, and he didn't want to make a spectacle of himself in front of my mother.

So instead of kneeling, my father just squatted down and stayed perched on his toes. This worked well enough, but the prayer meeting was infernally long and, soon, his toes started to hurt. He tried to rest them by shifting his weight between his legs—first to the left, then the right, and so on, back and forth.

This little toe dance helped, but the praying went on longer and longer and, soon, my father's legs began to hurt, too.

At last, he lost his balance, slipped, and fell to his knees.

"The Lord has brought you down," the preacher cried. "Now pray for your soul."

He thrust a Bible in front of my father, and my father—or so the story goes—broke into tears. He told my mother his true identity, confessed his sins to the preacher, and declared for Christ, right then and there.

After that fateful day, Jesse James began attending church and studying the Bible—singing in the choir, even. He asked my mother to marry him and she consented. But he still had to get her father's—my grandfather's—permission, and White Man Runs His Life, it seems, still had some common sense left in him.

"What will happen to my daughter if the officers of the law come after you?" he said.

"I'd surrender myself and clear my name if I could," my father said. "But they'd lynch me straight away."

Needless to say, my grandfather still wouldn't approve the marriage, so my mother went to my grandmother for advice. As I said, Grandmother was a Blackfoot and, before Christianity came in, the tradition for Blackfoot couples, when their parents didn't approve of the mates they'd selected, was to go ahead and elope, anyway. The couple would just go into the woods, come back a few days later and the parents would accept things.

"You can go off and elope like Blackfeet," my grandmother laughed. "But make sure you get married in a church first."

That was what they did. Just to make certain of things, my father gave my grandfather fifteen horses as a dowry. Nobody has ever told me how this poor wanderer obtained such an impressive remuda. If he was really who he claimed to be, it's not hard to guess.

"I'll work hard around here," he told my grandfather, when he presented him with the horses. "And when there's no ranch work to be done I'll do God's work."

After that, my father worked on the ranch during the week, then, on Sundays, rode around the territory and spread the Gospel. Everything was fine until he stumbled into the Catholic church where most of the service was in Latin.

"If people can't understand, what's the point of it?"

"The point is salvation."

"But wouldn't it be better if they could understand their salvation? Maybe what the church tells them is wrong."

"The church is infallible," the priest said—or, at least, that's what my mother says that the priest said.

After that, my father would go to that same Catholic church every Sunday and stand outside and preach at the top of his lungs—shout the gospel in their ears, my mother used to say. The priest didn't like it very much—having some lunatic screaming on his doorstep every Sunday—and summoned the sheriff, who drove my father off.

"I ought to kill him," he told my mother.

My mother shook her head. "You will not break God's command."

My father broke down in tears. "It's the same as always. I'll be hunted and hounded and, soon, you'll be hunted and hounded, too."

My mother told him to put his faith in God.

"Yes," he said, "God called on me to spread His word, and God will show the way."

Noble sounding words, but the facts are that, shortly after my mother became pregnant with me, my father abandoned her.

The story goes that God wanted him to convert the Indians, so he went to the Nez Perce reservation in Washington. He was supposed to return to us when his mission was completed, but he never did. I do recall my mother getting some letters from him when I was a very little boy, but, whatever the truth of his origins, I can never forgive him for what he did to us.

Was he really Jesse James? Well, I doubt that. But my mother believes that he was, and I think the most sensible explanation for the whole affair is that she married—or was seduced by—some fellow named Dave Woods, who—for reasons I'll never know—enjoyed passing himself off as the great outlaw.

A few years ago, I went to Colville, Washington, where my father is said to have died, and I made some inquiries. The logical places to start were the churches, and I met a preacher who said he remembered Dave Woods. He said Woods had done some good works in the area in the eighties, but that he didn't know what had become of him after that.

"Did he ever say anything to the effect that he was really Jesse James?" I said.

"Jesse James?" the preacher exclaimed. He shook his head. "Jesse James was killed a long time before that. It's not possible for Dave Woods to have been Jesse James."

"But didn't you know? Jesse James rose from the dead a week after they buried him."

The preacher laughed in my face. "That's the most ridiculous thing I ever heard."

42

September 1882
Colonel Jax Brown, Representative, Missouri State
Legislature
Letter to Frank James

My Dear Frank,

My apologies for not having answered your dispatches sooner, but I have been laying wreathes at the shrine of Bacchus, and an awful trip it was. I promise I shall worship no more until matters are taken care of.

An arrangement, such as the one you describe, can certainly be made. It will take time, but if you are patient, I can assure you that no lynch mob will ever lay hands on you. You will surrender to the governor personally. After that, you will have to stand trial but, trust me, you need not fear a conviction.

I know you are anxious, but I can do nothing more to hasten things along. The governor has always been more Union and railroad than loyal and Democratic. Worse, I am no longer what I once was. Keats and others I dare not name work for you, now, and behind the scenes. Even so, they must divorce themselves from me for fear it would be held against you in the highest circles.

Our larger dreams grow more fleeting by the hour. We fought all our lives. We never surrendered. The rest is best forgotten.

Yours, Through and Beyond Death,

Jax Brown

43

August 1883
Three Articles from

THE NEW YORK EMPIRIC

1

THE FRANK JAMES TRIAL

__✶__

The Arrival of Mrs. Rhawn and Miss Ford
General Keats Makes a Fool of Himself

After numerous delays, the trial of Frank James for train robbery and murder began today in Gallatin, Daviess County, Missouri.

For days the hotels have been jammed with reporters, ex-rebels and various state officials intent on witnessing the trial. Yesterday, the country people began arriving—in wagons, buggies, and on horseback—adding more confusion to the scene. By eleven o'clock, when the trial was scheduled to begin, the courthouse square was so crowded with people that Judge Good saw fit to postpone the proceedings so they could be moved to the Opera House where more spectators could be accommodated.

Still, a ticket is almost impossible to come by.

When Frank James at last appeared, he was in the company of Colonel J. A. X. Brown, Representative of Eaton County, and a loud hurrah went up from the assembled crowd.

James, who seemed quite collected as he received the accolades of the ex-rebels in attendance, wore a conservative business suit and looked more the local haberdasher than a man accused of robbing a train and gunning down the conductor in cold blood.

It is said that Colonel Brown handpicked James's council, the best the South has to offer, and that James's council, in turn, handpicked the jury. While such rumors remain unproven, it cannot be denied that a half-dozen of the jurors are noted ex-Confederates and all are staunch Democrats.

Other rumors circulated by the most reliable of sources, say that the governor, in attempting to mend his political fences, has more or less guaranteed that James will not spend a day in jail even if convicted. It is said that the governor told James that he cannot pardon him before he has been convicted of a crime, but that he can do so afterwards, if necessary.

This morning Mrs. Mary Rhawn—reputed to have been either the lover of Jesse James, Pony Sawyer, or both—arrived in town and was lodged in the Occidental Hotel as a witness for the prosecution. Her storied beauty and the flamboyant dress of velvet and satin she wore, caused a great commotion among the ladies.

Just as Mrs. Rhawn entered the hotel, Miss Dora Ford—also reputed to have been either the lover of Jesse James, Pony Sawyer, or both—was leaving, and the onlookers gasped in anticipation as their paths crossed. But to the dismay of the crowd, not a word, not even a look of recognition, passed between the two women.

It is Pony Sawyer, himself—the jailbird, horse thief, and informer—who will be the prosecution's key witness. He was an accomplice at the Winston robbery and several others perpetrated by the Jameses but has been granted full immunity for his testimony. He appeared on the streets today with two heavy revolvers strapped to his waist, bragging that he will not let Jesse's friends do to him what was done to Everett Russell—who was murdered in 1880, after he informed on and attempted to assassinate Jesse James.

General Sidney Marion Keats, that distinguished ex-rebel, has been making himself appear less distinguished with each passing hour. Last night he was eating supper with certain important friends at the Colby House Hotel when he noticed a man at one of the tables who bore a remarkable resemblance to Pony Sawyer.

The General would doubtless have realized that the man wasn't Pony Sawyer if his vision had not been clouded by strong drink. As it was, the General rose from his table and strode to that of the unfortunate look-alike. Once there, he proceeded to deliver a stirring denunciation of informers and traitors to his frightened and confused victim. He concluded his remarks by challenging the man to a duel and drawing a revolver.

Only the intervention of Sheriff Johnny P. Graham prevented an awful tragedy from taking place.

2

THE TRIAL OF THE BANDIT-KING

— ☆ —

The Prisoner Stoical

— ☆ —

Pony Sawyer's Story

The opera house, where Frank James stands trial for robbery and murder, is always filled to capacity with gallant gentlemen and fashionable ladies. Judge Good, chivalrous to the core, has ordered Sheriff Graham to find seats for the ladies even if it is necessary to eject males who hold valid tickets.

Frank James, himself, sits with his back turned to the audience, paying little mind to colorful pageant that goes on around him. He listens, makes copious notes, never frowns or smiles and, upon occasion, holds whispered conferences with his attorneys.

Yesterday, the engineer, the messenger, and the baggage master of the Winston train gave their testimony.

Today, a passenger, John L. Collins, a stone mason from Colfax, Iowa, recounted the murders of John Billings, the conductor, and James Kroft, another passenger.

He said that while Conductor Billings was taking his ticket, four men entered the coach armed with revolvers. One of them rushed at Billings shouting obscenities, and the conductor, in fright, ran out onto the platform of the car. Collins heard shots fired and, from his window, saw Billings's body roll into a ditch.

Collins' friend, James Kroft, went to the door of the coach, looked out to see what was happening, and was shot in the head and killed. The audience in the court gasped in horror as Collins indicated, with a finger, where the bullet entered his friend's brain and told of the blood and gore that covered the platform.

Collins, however, was unable to identify Frank James as one of the three men who killed Kroft and the conductor, and it was left to prosecutor Wallace Van Gorder to prove that he was.

The next witness called was Pony Sawyer, who narrated the circumstances by which he became a member of Jesse James' band of robbers.

"Jesse's idea," Sawyer said, "was to work with smaller numbers than he had before. He figured this would lessen the chance of someone turning traitor and also mean there'd be fewer men to share the loot."

He described the train robbery in detail but said he did not see who killed the conductor and passenger. Then, he recounted a conversation between the defendant and his brother that occurred as they rode away from the scene of the crime.

Frank remarked, "I believe we killed two this time."

"Two, was it?" Jesse said. "I thought it was three."

"I can answer for one," Frank said, "the conductor."

"I saw a fellow peeping through the door," Jesse said, "so I shot him dead."

This testimony seemed to shake Frank James to the core. Now, instead of holding his head high, as he had done before, he presented a hang-dog and dejected appearance. By the time Sawyer's testimony ended, James fidgeted in his chair and bothered his counsel every few moments with useless suggestions. Men who know him say he is losing his grip.

3

THE TRIAL OF FRANK JAMES
— ☆ —
The Defendant Breaks Under Cross-Examination

It appears that Frank James's attorneys made a serious mistake by allowing him to testify in his own behalf. At first, under direct questioning, he seemed to tell a glib and smooth story, but when Wallace Van Gorder, the bespectacled, young prosecutor, took up the cross-examination, James was caught in a thousand contradictions. Afterwards, it seemed apparent to most unprejudiced listeners that his testimony was nothing more than a poorly constructed pack of lies.

Van Gorder: "Mr. James, unless you wanted to get back into robbing and killing, why did you leave Nashville with your brother?"

James: "I only went with Jesse to convince him not to go back to Missouri. I did not want another grenade thrown through our mother's window, and I told him so. But I only went with him as far as the Rhawn's in Kentucky. I never went with him to Missouri."

Van Gorder: "But earlier you said you were in Missouri after visiting the Rhawn's."

James: "I meant I was only passing through Missouri on my way to Texas. Missouri is between Kentucky and Texas, roughly. (Laughter from the courtroom) I never agreed to rob anything when I was at the Rhawn's. I was a man at peace."

Van Gorder: "Then why did you need so many weapons?"

James: "I had pistols but no rifle. I owned a rifle but my wife had it. When I went armed I only carried two pistols.

Van Gorder: "Do 'men at peace' always carry two pistols?"

Later, in a piece of masterful cross-examination, Mr. Van Gorder questioned the defendant regarding places he claimed to have been between the robbery at Winston and the robbery at Blue Cut. By the time he was done, it was clear that James had really been in Missouri, riding, as of old, in the heart of his brother's gang.

Van Gorder: "In Dennison, Texas, you say you bought a horse off the street from a man you didn't know?"

James: "That is correct."

Van Gorder: "Since you cannot recall the name of the man you bought the horse from, perhaps you could tell us who owned the ranch you stayed at that night."

James: "I don't recall it."

Van Gorder: "Perhaps you could describe the ranch for us?"

James: "I've stayed at many ranches. I don't recall any particulars."

Van Gorder: "And you don't recall whether it was south or east or west of Dennison."

James: "No, but the next night I stopped at a house that was near a creek."

Van Gorder: "But you still cannot describe any house at which you stayed well enough for anyone to find it, and you cannot name anyone with which you stayed or talked."

James: "I refuse to answer that question."

When James's testimony was done, the ex-rebels in the audience attempted to raise a demonstration in his behalf, but Judge Good and the marshals silenced it.

Tomorrow, the closing speeches are set to begin, and it is predicted they will run for several days. The defense, it is said, will emphasize James's life in Tennessee, and how he toiled, as a teamster, to make an honest living from 1877 to 1881. On the other hand, they will characterize Pony Sawyer as a horse thief and accomplice to murder—the man who cast the body of Tot Rhawn into an empty room in December of 1881, then opened the windows to the cold so he and the Fords could enjoy a pleasant game of cards, free from the stench of death.

44
March 1885
Colonel Jax Brown, Representative, Missouri State Legislature
Letter to Frank James

My Dear Frank,

I write to put your fears to rest. I fixed things for you at Gallatin and, now, I have fixed them everywhere.

You know that the governor and I have not been friends since I was obligated by honor to take sides against him, but I have finally managed to win him over. When I see you, I will tell you the whole of it, but the backs of your enemies have been broken. I swear that you will never again have to stand trial. Not in Missouri, not in Minnesota, not even in Hell, if I can manage it.

We fought many fights together and now the last is done. We were overwhelmed by sheer weight of numbers, and it is a pity for the world.

Things were once so beautiful. We could have accomplished so many great things. The Romans and Greeks would have been as nothing compared to the civilization we might have built.

I know it is best to forget, but I find I cannot. Instead, I remember a world where excellent men did excellent things. Now, we are left with a tyranny of equality that reduces everyone to the lowest form and makes all things common and ugly.

Poor Jesse. Oh, what a manly fellow. Thank God you are safe. Lay low. Stay quiet. Try to forget. There are things that courage alone cannot change.

Yours, Through and Beyond Death
Jax Brown

45
Spring 1892
Parzival Hartwig, Saloon Keeper
Denver, Colorado

People tell lots of bad stories about Bob Ford, but I don't believe them. They say he ran the gangs in Creede, but all he ever run was a saloon, far as I know. He had some pimps, but pimps are as common as dogs in boomtowns.

I come to Creede in March of ninety-two because the mines were rich and there was money all over. The trains going there were packed full, but the town wasn't much. It sprawled out along a little valley between two big cliffs—one long street of saloons, gambling halls, and cribs.

The citizens had put in electric arc lamps along the sidewalks which made the night seem like day, a thing I found amusing. But prices were sky high and a cot to sleep on for a night cost two dollars.

Bat Masterson had a saloon, and one night he caught me trying to catch forty winks by the stove. He didn't kick me out but bought me a beer, instead.

He asked me what my name was and when I told him, I got the usual reaction. I told him people usually called me Hart.

"Where do you come from?" he asked.

"Hall County, Nebraska. Near Grand Island."

He asked me how old I was.

"Old enough," I told him.

"You ought to be at home raising corn."

"We breed sheep."

"Well, you still ought to be back there."

I shook my head but didn't tell him why.

It was like this—my father had always wanted me to take over the farm, I being his oldest son and him having homesteaded the place. But when I was sixteen I was weary of life among the sheep and I wanted to go adventuring. I told my father I wanted to learn what the world was like.

"You'll learn what it's like to starve," he said, which was one of the longer conversations I ever held with him.

He kept his money buried under the hearth in a cookie jar and one morning, before the rooster crowed, I got into it. I took half for myself and left a note which explained that I'd only took what I deserved. Then I made me a lunch and walked all the way to Grand Island.

Grand Island was a division point on the railroad and a bustling place. I had always desired to ride a train, having seen them running through the fields like great iron horses, as they are called. So, I snuck into the yards and hopped a freight heading west.

But when I got to Denver a railroad bull busted me on the noggin and robbed me of the money I'd robbed from my father. After that, I did anything I could to keep body and soul from separating, including boxing, and by the time I got to Creede, my nose and ears looked like cauliflower.

Masterson asked me what my ambitions were, and I told him I had it in mind to get some girls and have them earn money for me.

"No girls are going to go with you," Masterson said. "Why would any girls go with you?"

"My good looks?" I laughed.

He told me he was staging boxing matches on the side, and that one glance at my nose and missing teeth told him I had some experience in the ring.

"I give my boys five dollars appearance money," he told me, "and fifty more if they win."

Those were handsome terms compared to others I'd fought for. I told him I'd do it, and on the very next night, I had my inaugural fight in Creede.

The matches were held in a big tent that some church people from Denver had put up. Masterson offered them twenty-five percent of the take to put on "sparing exhibitions"—which would be fought with gloves instead of bareknuckles—and since everyone, even the righteous, needed money in Creede, the church people agreed.

On fight nights, waiters in mustaches and long, white aprons carried big trays of beer in glass mugs up and down the aisles. Cigar smoke filled the air and everything smelled of sweat and whiskey. Masterson, himself, acted as referee, dispensing judgments with which no one argued, for no one dared cross a man with his reputation.

The man I was paired against that first night didn't know much about the boxing art. He never touched me. I put him down a number of times, but he was game and kept getting up. The crowd always likes that, and so there was lots of cheering for him and booing of me. It didn't do him much good, though.

After a few more fights I got to be known and respected around Creede, in it's watering holes and gambling houses. Men would buy me drinks and praise me. But it's never a good idea to train with one foot on a bar-rail, and a fortnight later, I went up against a man named Paddy Bragan and learned a lesson.

He was lightly built but very fast. We were dancing around, but not accomplishing much, which made the crowd sullen. Then, in a flash, this Bragan lashed out and tagged me with a straight-right dead in the center of the forehead.

When it hit, I thought, "That didn't hurt much."

But he threw again without hesitation. This time, I saw the punch coming. But I couldn't move my hands, and he hit me square between the eyes once more.

This time I thought, "This is bad."

He hit me a third time, and again I was frozen and could do nothing. The fourth time he hit me, I was already on the way down.

I saw stars for about two days after, and the next time I fought the same thing happened. I got hit in the head and the blow seemed to cleave thought from action.

Masterson told me, "You won't have any brains left if you keep on fighting."

"I have to eat," I told him. "I don't want to go into the mines. I can't breathe in close spaces."

"You could go back to Nebraska."

I told him about me stealing my father's money and he shook his head with sadness. "Some things you never stop paying for."

He thought for a moment. "I hear Bob Ford is looking for a bouncer and a bodyguard. Maybe you'd like that."

Bob Ford had a saloon and gambling hall, like Masterson's. He always had money and the best clothes— wearing the same bright colors and checkered patterns that I favored.

"There's nobody trying to kill him that I know of," Masterson said.

I told him the job seemed like a good idea, so he took me over to Ford's. Bob had seen me fight so no introductions were necessary.

"When men get drunk," he said, "they sometimes try to pick a quarrel with me."

"They won't when I'm around," I told him.

"Do you believe I'm a Judas, like the stories say?"

I thought for a moment. "Yes, I suppose I do."

"Judas just played his part," Bob said. "If it wasn't for Judas, Jesus wouldn't have been crucified, and there wouldn't be any salvation. Did you ever think of that?"

"No," I said, "I guess I never listened much in Sunday school."

He laughed and gave me the job, then took me around to meet his girls.

He only had two at the time. One was a mulatto girl called Jolly—tall and pretty—who had joined up with him when he had a saloon in New Mexico. She was from Texas and wore cowboy boots which made her even taller. She ran the dice game and had a manner about her that drew in the customers. I admired her from the start.

"What the hell kind of a name is Parzival Hartwig?" she asked me.

"German," I told her. "People usually call me Hart."

"Well, I'll call you Parzy," she said, and that's what she's called me ever since.

The other girl, Opal, was no good. There was morphine all over in Creede—cheaper than whiskey—and Opal was on it. Bob sometimes fooled around with her, but he had a wife he loved so this Opal was just temporary with him. He wouldn't have took up with no addict permanent.

Later on, I met his wife. Her name was Lucy, and she'd been an actress, back east. She was fair-haired and very pretty, but she seemed out of her element in Creede. She stayed in their apartments, upstairs above the saloon, most of the time. Bob always talked about making a big strike, taking her to New York and getting her on the stage.

"You know I don't care about that," she'd say to Bob.

She was always very nice to me. She would joke and say, "My, for such a big boy, you do make the best doughnuts." That was one of my jobs, making coffee and doughnuts.

"You'll make some girl a wonderful husband, some day."

"Parzy?" Jolly would laugh. "Somebody's husband?"

I still tease her about that.

About a month after I started working in the saloon, a man Bob had known from Missouri come in. Bob was very happy to see him and the two got drunk together. That night, they shot up the town very bad, breaking windows and street lamps all over. There wasn't any real law in Creede, but the vigilance men got up in arms over this and Bob decided to go to Pueblo for his health.

When he was there, the hotels were all very crowded and he ended up sharing a room with the fellow who later killed him—Virgil Dailey, his name was. I don't know exactly what happened in Pueblo, but I think it was like this.

Bob had just come into some money—I don't know about that, either. But when he was in Pueblo, Bob bought a big diamond ring for his wife, and it so happened the ring disappeared the night he stayed with Virgil Dailey.

When the vigilance men in Creede settled down, Bob came back. He was very mad about the ring being stolen and told everybody in town that Dailey was a thief.

"I bought it for you," he said to Lucy.

She seemed very upset. "I don't care about diamonds."

On the day Bob was killed, Dailey came into the saloon acting very angry and impertinent.

"Tell your boss he'd better stop spreading lies about me."

The bartender and I jumped him and knocked him down. We took a pistol off him and threw him out.

When Bob came in, I told him about it.

"I'm not afraid of any sneak thief," he said.

When Dailey came back he was wearing a long coat, even though the weather was fair. It should have tipped me off, but it all happened too fast.

Bob was dealing Faro. I was back of the bar. Jolly was running her dice game, and Opal, the other girl, was just sitting and drinking. Dailey came in the swinging doors. I looked at him. He pulled a shotgun from under his coat. I should have done something, but it was like when Paddy Bragan hit me.

"Hey, Bob," he said.

Bob looked up, and Dailey fired. Opal started screaming.

Dailey run out, but I didn't go after him. Instead, I picked Bob up and put him on the card-table. His blood ran all over. I tried to stop it with my handkerchief, but it was hopeless. One of his collar buttons was lodged in his throat from the gun blast, and I tried to dig it out with my fingers.

"Oh, Jesus," I said.

Jolly pulled my hand away.

"Leave him be."

I tried to tell Bob I was sorry. It looked like he wanted to say something, but his windpipe was cut, and he was already dead.

Lucy come running down the stairs. When she saw Bob on the table, she flung herself at Opal. Jolly and I pulled her off.

That night, Opal took too much morphine, went to sleep, and never woke up.

After that, I'd had enough of boomtowns. When I left, Lucy paid me everything Bob owed me, and I was very grateful. I tried to apologize once more for his death.

"I should have done something," I said.

"It wasn't your fault."

When I said goodbye to Masterson, I tried to tell him how I felt about it. "I saw the gun come out, but I was frozen and couldn't move."

He shrugged his shoulders. "Some things are just written in the stars."

I bumped into Jolly at the depot. The platform was crowded because the trains going back to the world were the ones that were full, now. Jolly was sitting on her baggage in the sun and I thought I had never seen so beautiful a sight.

"Going back to Nebraska, Parzy?" she asked.

"No," I told her. "I don't regard that as ever possible. Denver is where I'm going."

"Me, too," Jolly said. "Maybe we ought to throw in together."

"Maybe so," I said, and I haven't been able to get rid of her since.

46
May 1893
Aldus Chiles, Convicted Murderer
Minnesota State Prison
Letters to Evangeline Nyborg

Sunday, May 7, 1893
Dear Miss Nyborg,

I have the most sanguine news, and it is due, in no small measure, to your kind exertions on my behalf. Reverend Thielman has at long last agreed to post my letters to you, and because of this I no longer need moderate what I say. Happily, he has also agreed to deliver your letters to me, so in the future, be so kind as to send them in his care, to his address. You cannot possibly know how much they mean to me.

Almost as extraordinary, is the news that the Reverend has succeeded in his other endeavor, and I am no longer required to perform the menial duties that only seem to be assigned to colored prisoners— the cleaning and scrubbing of the cellhouse floor, the whitewashing of the cells, the endless attempts to exterminate the bedbugs that infest this place.

I now labor in the prison library, as I have desired to do for so long. My imprisonment has spanned sixteen years thus far—hours upon hours, alone in a cell—and the reading of books—any and every sort of book—is the only thing that has kept me sane.

But never did I imagine how beautiful a place our little library might be. In the very front of it, there is a big bay window that overlooks the prison street where we march on Sundays—our only exercise. But oak trees line this otherwise grim arterial and, from my window, I can see them in all their greenery.

And more, there is a little book bindery that adjoins the library and what is in it? A birdcage that hangs from the ceiling and is inhabited by two energetic canaries. There are even potted plants. You cannot imagine what it is like to hear birds sing, to water plants, to be surrounded by books—endless, wonderful books, exuding dust and the aroma of yellowing pages.

Jim Younger, of the famous outlaw brothers, also works in the library. He is bald and middle-aged and seems to have some difficulty, or pain, about the face and jaw. We are allowed to speak, but only concerning the management of the library and only when circumstance demands. Even though we are called "trustees," a screw always watches.

Ten years ago, in the dead of night, there were fires. The wood shop, went up and two store houses. The cellhouse itself caught fire and there was panic. Anarchy reigned, many could have escaped, but the Youngers, like Judas-goats, helped the screws herd us outside the burning walls.

In the silence of the library, I slipped a note into a book and passed it to Younger.

"Nero fiddled while Rome burned. Why didn't you run?"

He understood at once and wrote back, "We hope for parole."

Once, I escaped for two days, and, for those two days, I was again human. It was winter, and I almost froze, but such exhilaration, such joy.

In solitary, they starve you. They stand you up and chain your wrists to the bars of the cell door, and that is how you stay all day—chained, standing. There is an outer iron door just beyond the bars, and they close that, too, so when you are chained you see nothing but the iron bars and the iron door, solid as doom.

But once a week, for fifteen minutes, they let you take a bath, unchained, and it is sheer bliss. Those two days of my escape were like those fifteen minutes but magnified a thousand fold. Imagine, Miss Nyborg—fifteen minutes, two days.

God Bless and Keep You.

Your Obedient Servant
Aldus Chiles

⌘

Sunday, May 21, 1893
Dear Miss Nyborg,

Reverend Thielman brought me your letter today. I was so thrilled to see it, I tore it open while he stood in my cell.

You ask what I did to deserve the awful torture of solitary. I answer, everything and nothing—for being dilatory, for defacing property, for breaking the rule of silence, for spitting, stealing, quarreling, for the crime of being colored. But I have learned to fool the screws, now, so I have not undergone such punishment for almost two years.

A week ago Friday, in the dark night of the cellhouse, high on the sixth tier, a man woke screaming. It is a thing that happens with great regularity. But this fellow was a Russian immigrant and harmless. He screamed that the bedbugs were biting him. He screamed that he was being consumed alive and that he would kill the warden. The screws climbed the tiers and tormented him. You could hear them laughing and the men in the cells began to shout, demanding they stop. Several were beaten and dragged away.

Reverend Thielman said he would see what he could do.

"Christ would have died for them," I said.

"I am not Christ," he replied.

I once held a conversation with the Reverend in which we compared the existence in solitary to that of the hermit monks of the middle ages—those creatures who sought the desert, walled themselves into tiny cells, ate almost nothing, and prayed on their knees until they were blessed with hallucinations.

In solitary it is like that. You are fed only bread and water. You stand, chained to the bars. The screws are supposed to unchain you at night, but sometimes one of them takes a dislike to you and won't let you down. So you hang, crucified like Christ, praying like a hermit monk, and when you have hung long enough and starved long enough—for days, for weeks—you have visions, mirages that shimmer in the desert of the mind.

My father was a preacher in Jefferson County, near Louisville, in Kentucky. We lived, like mice, in the back of his church—an old, decrepit, colored church. I slept on a porch that was screened in summer and shuttered in winter. The graveyard lay just beyond my door and in my dreams the corpses, as on Judgment Day, rose up and walked. In the stillness of a summer night, whenever the crickets fell silent, I would think the corpses were coming and I would hide under my bed.

In solitary, when I was chained for months to the bars. The people I'd killed came in through the walls of my cell. I wept when my wife and children appeared and, as I did, they became angelic spirits. I was ecstatic—an exhilaration like Christ must have felt on the Cross, the beatitude of martyrdom.

"Father, forgive them."

When the screws came to unchain me, I was in such bliss from my visions, that I refused to lay down on the wooden plank they call a bed. Instead, I stayed up at the bars, my hands grasping them as they had all day, and for this, I was beaten.

Today, in the library, when the screw was looking out the bay window, I passed another note to Jim Younger.

"You don't really think they'll parole you."

"We have friends, but also enemies."

"Why don't I see you in the trustee's dining room?"

"Shot in the jaw when captured. Can't take solid food. Eat in my cell. Don't like to be seen eating."

"Do you feel sorry for yourself?"

"Yes."

*I watch him. He keeps to himself. He reads about spiritualism and theosophy—Mme. Blavatsky, **Isis Unveiled,** and **Atlantis**, by Ignatius Donnelly. He is, as I once was when I still had hope.*

I dared whisper to him. "Why do you work for them?"

He was frightened, but the ecstasy of speaking—the sweet danger of it—swept him along.

"For the same reason you do," he said.

"To escape?"

"In my own way."

233

Reverend Thielman defines freedom as the freedom to obey God's rule—a handy perspective for a lackey of the screws. For a time, I found freedom in books. Younger thinks he will find it by cutting himself off from the material world, dwelling close to the spirits and hoping for better in the next incarnation.

Maybe he is right. I cannot account for what I did to my wife and children. I remember wanting to end their pain.

But sometimes the warden, the deputy warden, the doctor—the most self-important of the screws—use Negroes as house servants. One of them, a coachman for the warden, just drove off one day and disappeared. The screws say he was recaptured, but I don't believe them.

That is why I indulge in this hypocritical subterfuge of being a trustee. That is why I debase myself and shuffle along with eyes downcast—for the chance to get outside the gates of this place to be beyond its evil turrets and bastions.

Listen. My own brief escape was a thing of such beauty. Every morning they wake us at 5:30 to march us to breakfast. In winter, it is still very dark at that hour and, one day, when the screws marched us out, I hid. There was nothing more to it than that. When they were gone, I slipped out after them, made my way to the wall—to the railroad gate, which isn't very tall—and went right on over.

I know of two other escapes—that of a man who actually sawed through the bars, and that of two other men who simply ran out the wagon gate when it opened to let a team go out.

Then, too, there is the most desperate escape of all—the death dive from the sixth tier of the cellhouse. Four men have leaped since I've been here—one of them somehow survived.

"Maybe the angels bore him up," Reverend Thielman said.

Imagine, Miss Nyborg, the sheer ecstasy as you soar down and then live, as if by a miracle.

*If you could somehow get me a copy of **Utopia**, by Thomas More, I would be ever so grateful. Reverend Thielman says it is a socialist book and refuses to buy such a thing for me. But in his heart he struggles with Christ. I know he will smuggle it in if you give it to him. There is no way I can pay you, but there is no danger for you, either. I can hide the book on the shelves in the library. It is perfect. The screws are too stupid to ever find it.*

God Bless and Keep You
Your Obedient Servant
Aldus Chiles

⌘

Sunday, June 4, 1893
Dear Miss Nyborg,

Last Tuesday was Decoration Day and on such holidays we prisoners are allowed to mingle and even speak in a little park that stands inside the walls.

It is lovely there with mowed grass and trees. In the midst of it stands a little bandstand from which our prison band, a brass band, plays. Civil War songs were played in honor of the day. The warden made a trivial speech and the screws, in all their fine mercy, gave us an extra ration of tobacco in honor of the dead.

We smoked our riches with abandon and clustered in little groups—ants at a picnic. There are not many coloreds here, but, as is advisable, I stayed with "my own kind," for the most part. But when I noticed Jim Younger and his brother, Cole, lying on the grass in the sun, carrying on a jovial conversation—remembering better times, perhaps—I went up to them, squatted on my haunches, and said hello.

Jim introduced me to Cole, who was polite, but aloof. He, like Jim, is balding and middle-aged but respected here by the strength of his reputation. He fidgeted and gnawed on the stem of his pipe as the band played "John Brown's Body." He did not like the song, and I believe he was uncomfortable in the presence of a Negro.

"Prison ain't so bad," he said, "if you don't fight it. You go along with the authorities. As a river rolls, so do you."

"It's different for you," I told him. "You have friends. You have money."

"Only a little," Cole said.

"A little goes a long way in a place like this."

Jim said, "Money and friends haven't done us much good so far."

Cole admonished him. "These things take time."

"It's been fifteen years," Jim told me. "Our brother had consumption, and they wouldn't even let him out to die. They'll never let us out."

"Maybe you ought to let yourselves out."

Cole shook his head. "Impossible and foolish. We'd just get captured or killed."

"And what if we were?" Jim said. "At least it would be over."

"You've got to keep your courage up. We have friends. We'll get paroled one day."

"One day when?"

Thank you ever so much for Utopia, Miss Nyborg. I gave the book to Younger and he at once loved it. But I must ask another favor. Could you please get me a copy of Edward Bellamy's **Looking Backward?** It is a book that is proscribed here and, although I have read about it and the glorious utopian community it describes, I have never been able to even glimpse the book itself. Again, I cannot pay you, but, if you do procure it, it would be most wonderful if you could deliver it in person. You cannot know what seeing you again would mean to me.

May the Universal God Keep You
Your Obedient Servant
Aldus Chiles

⌘

Sunday, June 18, 1893
Dear Miss Nyborg,

You are wrong in what you say.

I have asked for books, yes, but I am not trying to take advantage of you. You say I asked for money but I never did. All I said was that money could buy many things and that is the truth. I asked you to come visit me, but that does not mean I have romantic longings. I dream of darker things, gods and ghosts.

Younger dreams of a horse ranch. How quaint. He dreams of his girl back in Missouri, and of flying. He dreams that the angels will bear *him up, but he is a fool. It is all chance —to be born rich, to be born poor—a vast and hilarious joke. The screws roll the dice and laugh.*

I will keep writing, no matter what you say or do. If Reverend Thielman will no longer carry the letters, I will send them through the regular post. If you do not reply, I will still write. You women are all the same. Don't even think of betraying me.

Your Obedient Servant
Aldus Chiles

47
July 1894
THE WEEKLY HUMBUG
Santa Rosa, California

TWO IS ONE TOO MANY
A Curious Happening at Garth & Carp's

Among the more popular exhibits at Garth & Carp's Amusement Gardens in Rio Nido, is one featuring a man who is alleged to be the notorious outlaw Jesse James. When interviewed by your reporter in May, this man told a convincing story and was unerring in relating the events that occurred in the life of the famed outlaw. He seemed to be about the right age and, in appearance, seemed sturdy enough to have once led the outlaw life.

Mr. Garth, of the Gardens, as we then reported, met the alleged Jesse on the Duck Valley Indian reservation in Nevada almost a year ago and, before bringing him to California, did all that was humanly possible to ascertain the truth of his story.

Garth believed, thoroughly and completely, that this man was in fact, Jesse James, and this newspaper was inclined towards believing it too, at least until the events of last Sunday night.

The evening began in the usual fashion at Garth & Carp's. There was music and gaiety. The games on the midway were attended by a throng of vacationers, and Jesse James, the Jesse on exhibit that is, was shaking hands with patrons when another man, about the same age and build, came up to him.

"You're a liar," this second fellow exclaimed.

Mrs. Ida Lilly, staying at River Bend for the summer, said Jesse's accuser was in the company of a woman with two young children and that he appeared to be under the influence of spirits. She says his woman companion attempted to get him away from the James exhibit but failed, and that he produced a pistol from a shoulder holster and swung it in the direction of Mr. Garth's Jesse.

"To the devil with you, sir. I am Jesse James and you are a poltroon."

Mrs. Lilly was unable to relate much of what happened next for she, like most of the patrons, was more interested in saving her life. Another witness, Homer Jensen, who runs Garth's bowling alley, ducked behind one of the wooden benches that sit in front of the Rose Gardens.

He peeked out, hoping to see some shooting, only to discover that the first Jesse was leaving the field of honor at the best possible speed.

"You had better run, you dog," the second Jesse shouted.

The first Jesse has not been seen since, but informants have told us that the second is a man known to them as Clay J. Davis. We learned, also, that he was renting a cottage among the Germans at River Grove and, in seeking to determine which Jesse, if either, was the real one, we took the excursion train there and made some inquiries.

Mr. Rudolph Mueller, who owns the River Grove Cabins, told us that Mr. Davis and his family had, indeed, been vacationing there, but that they had departed in haste that very morning.

When apprised of the incident at Garth & Carp's, Mr. Mueller said he was thoroughly in the dark. Davis, he said, had introduced himself as a horse breeder from Napa and a member of the Odd Fellows Lodge. His wife, Alma, was a German girl, much younger than Davis and aged about twenty-two. Their children, Mr. Mueller said, were aged about three and four years and seemed well behaved.

We then journeyed to Napa where we inquired at the Odd Fellows Lodge about this man and, after some demurring, were given his address. Upon arriving there we found his wife to be as described. Alas, Mr. Davis was unavailable for comment.

His wife told us that he was suffering from melancholia. She said he had been dejected over business reverses for sometime and that they had taken their cabin at River Grove under doctor's advice, hoping the cooler weather would do him some good. It was nerves, she said, that caused him to put on the display at Garth & Carp's.

"The James Boys have been something of a hobby of his for sometime. He collects memorabilia about them and was merely incensed by the fraud he saw at the amusement park."

She added that they have been considering moving to San Francisco and going into the bakery business with her uncle. She said they will probably do so as soon as her husband's health improves. We were tempted to tell her that there was an opening he might be suited for at the Amusement Gardens, but—as she had already closed the door in our faces—we were not at liberty to pursue the subject.

48
May 1896
THE ST. LOUIS UNION

FRANK JAMES TURNS THESPIAN
— ✩ —
His Views on His Brother

The Opera House at Gallatin was thronged to capacity last night for the opening of Mr. Milton LeGrow's production of William Shakespeare's Richard III. It turned out to be a passably good blood and thunder epic, filled with murder, conspiracy, war, and poison. But despite it's relentless action, the audience was most amused during those moments when a certain newcomer, portraying King Edward IV of England, trod the boards.

"My brother killed no man," the old king declaimed. "His fault was thought, and yet his punishment was bitter death..."

These lines brought down the house, most probably because they were recited by that illustrious ex-outlaw Frank James.

"It's the most receptive audience I've seen since I stood trial in 1883 in this very same auditorium," James said, later, as he sat in his dressing room removing his makeup.

"I've always admired the classics," he continued, "but I never knew acting would be so simple. I'd prefer playing leads, of course, but I suppose that will come in time."

Our reporter was less interested in James's career as an actor than in his earlier exploits on the stage of life. He enquired about James's wartime adventures but, alas, made the mistake of referring to that unpleasant period in our history as "The Civil War."

"I know of no war called by that name, young man," the old outlaw barked. "A number of years ago I fought in a war called the War for Southern Independence, but I know of no war that is properly called the Civil War."

Our reporter repaired his syntax and tried again.

"In the War for Southern Independence, it is my understanding that you rode with the notorious guerrilla fighter, Quantrill."

James, who was chewing tobacco, ruminated for a moment.

"Yes, I rode with Quantrill," he admitted at last. "People say he was an evil man—a man who loved death. But, listen, the love of death leads to the love of life, for such things reveal themselves as one. Yes, I rode with Quantrill. Yes, I descended into a labyrinth of war—like Theseus unto the Minotaur—but I found my way through the tangled passages and emerged, battered but stronger, a better man."

"There have been certain rumors," our reporter continued, "to the effect that your brother wasn't killed in St. Joseph, fourteen years ago, but that he is alive and well and living in Texas, Mexico or some other far flung place."

"People should never put stock in rumors," James said.

"Do you know for a fact that Jesse was killed by the Fords?"

"Well, I saw him in his coffin, I can tell you that. If it wasn't him they laid away then it was his twin brother, and I can say, for a fact, that Jesse James had no twin brother."

Recently, Frank and his mother have opened the family's old farm—the infamous Castle James—to tourists and our reporter, having been brought to the point of exasperation by the old outlaw's previous evasions, made a cynical inquiry.

"Do you refuse to squelch the rumors about Jesse's death simply to create more interest in your tourist business?"

"I don't like your tone of voice, young man. The Federals denied me a chance to make an honest living at war's end, and now you act as if you want to do the same. There's nothing wrong with selling souveniers to tourists. It's a legal occupation. If people want to purchase a pebble off Jesse's grave, or an autographed photo of myself, I'll not stand in their way."

"And the people prefer a live Jesse to a dead one?"

"Young man, the idea that my brother hatched some sort of plot to fake his own death is too absurd to contemplate. It is you fellows, the men of the press, who keep these rumors alive and without having one scintilla of evidence, I might add. You are the ones who profit from it, not I."

49

Spring 1903
Winfield "Skeeter" Griggs
Jackson County, Missouri

My brothers and I were the modern incarnation of the Younger Gang, or so we liked to think. We lived in Lee's Summit—Cole Younger's hometown—and Cole's sister, Louise Younger Runnels, lived right across the road from us. It was more than a boy could ask.

I remember a warm July evening when I was ten. My older brother, Samuel Tilden Griggs, was twelve. My little brother, Grover Cleveland Griggs, was a little sprout of seven. We'd gone up to Seery's barn with the idea of setting off firecrackers and giving the old fellow a scare, but our work was interrupted when a train whistle sounded in the distance—two shrill blasts, the order to release brakes. We never could pass up the temptation of a train, so we climbed up into the loft and from there we could see it—a slow freight, laboring its way towards Kansas City.

"Skeet," Sam exclaimed—people called me Skeeter even then. "It's laden down with pirate treasure. Treasure heading for the coffers of the north."

Grover and I dashed for the ladder that led down to the ground, but Sam stopped us.

"If we're going to rob a train, we've got to take the Robber's Oath."

Right there, in Seery's loft we pricked our fingertips with our pocketknives and pressed our hands together. We swore never to harm a workingman or a Southern woman. We swore never to betray a friend and to come to each other's aid, no matter what the consequences.

In those days we were all very certain we were destined for great things. Sam wanted to become rich. I wanted to be a baseball player. And while we were both quite sure we'd realize those ambitions, we had our doubts about Grover.

Grover, you see, wanted to ride with Jesse James, but Jesse was already dead.

In 1900, when Sam turned twenty, he got a job in St. Louis selling steam boiler insurance and did very well at it. But he never forgot our Robber's Oath, and in the summer of 1902, when he came back home to Lee's Summit for a visit, he brought a friend with him—a certain Mr. Gus Doljack, who worked for the St. Louis Browns baseball team, in the brand-new American League.

I was playing shortstop for our local nine, at the time, and was the highest paid player on the team at a dollar a game. Sam's visit just happened to coincide with our Fourth of July tilt against the boys from Raytown, and he brought Mr. Doljack to see me play.

I had four hits that day, made a couple of diving stops at short, and Mr. Doljack granted me a tryout with the Browns.

I ended up playing infield for the Browns, the White Sox, and the Indians from 1902 to 1908. You can look it up, as the saying goes. Skeeter Griggs, bats left, throws right, five feet five, one hundred twenty-eight pounds, lifetime batting average .228—the fulfillment of a dream.

Grover's dream—that of riding with the James Gang— began coming true just a year after mine did. For in 1903, with his two brothers dead—Bob having died of consumption in Stillwater Prison, and Jim having taken his own life—Cole Younger was at last pardoned and allowed to return home to his native state.

He came to live with his sister in Lee's Summit, right across the road from us. I couldn't be there for the big celebration—as I was with the Browns—so I didn't meet Cole until Grover's eighteenth birthday that fall. Cole was sixty years old, by then. He'd lost a lot of hair and become a bit portly—hardly the rough and tumble bear of a man he'd been when he was riding with Frank and Jesse. But he was still everything I'd imagined him to be.

"That's a nasty looking scar you've got," Cole said, as we shook hands on the porch.

The scar was under my right eye and had required twelve stitches. I'd committed two errors in one inning in my debut at short—five in the game all told—and our pitcher hadn't taken to kindly to it. Ballplayers were roughly hewn in those days, and this pitcher met me in an alley after the game and taught me a lesson.

But I wasn't about to tell Cole Younger I'd been beaten up by some baseball player—and a pitcher, of all things.

"A grounder got me," I told him. "Took a bad hop. They come like skyrockets when the dirt gets hard in summer."

Cole had taken to smoking a long, curving meerschaum pipe in prison, and he put it in his mouth, and chewed on it for a moment.

"I didn't know baseball was such a dangerous sport."

I tried to laugh it off, but Cole had seen right through my charade. After dinner, he dragged me out into the front yard and gave me some lessons in self-defense. Not the manly art of boxing, so-called, but that of using common items as weapons—house keys, belts, belt buckles, suspenders, shoes. You name it, Cole could turn it into a weapon.

But this was Grover's birthday celebration, as you'll recall, and it turned out that Cole had one heck of a present planned for my little brother. Right after we polished off the birthday cake and ice cream, Cole lit up that pipe of his.

"You know, Louise," he said to his sister, "I don't reckon its right for me to keep sponging off you like this."

"You're not sponging, Cole. Lord knows you deserve some peace after what you've been through."

"No. A man's got to pull his weight in this world. It seems Frank has grown tired of selling trinkets to the tourists and he's had a business offer."

He paused and we all fell silent. "Mr. Milton LeGrow, of Chicago, a theatrical man and an old friend of Frank's, wants to... well..."

He lifted his pipe, and pointed the stem at my little brother.

"Grover, how do you think you'd like working for a wild west show."

Grover must have jumped two feet out of his chair. "A wild west show? With Indians and Rough Riders and cowboys?"

"Yes," Cole said. "Mr. LeGrow thinks we might even have a balloon ascension."

"A balloon ascension?" his sister laughed. "What on earth do balloons have to do with the wild west?"

Cole shrugged. "Frank says, if the people want balloons, give them balloons."

Grover signed on right then and there, and all that winter he worked like a beaver for Mr. LeGrow and Cole and Frank. They signed up fifty riders, and Grover even discovered an actress and dancer in Kansas City—Miss Edna Alice Singer— who was willing to dress in flesh-colored tights and fly through space in the basket of a balloon.

The James/Younger Wild West Show opened in Independence the next spring. Grover sent me a free pass. Once again, I was with the Browns and couldn't make it. It was my second full season in the majors and my hopes were high. But the Browns had a fellow named Bobby Wallace at short and I spent most of the year shining the bench with the seat of my pants.

In 1905, the wild west show happened to be in St. Louis during one of our homestands. Frank, Cole and Grover came around to see our show, one day, and on the next, I rode the electric out to the fairgrounds to see their's. Grover was supervising the ticket sales when I arrived. A handful of cigars was stuffed in his breast pocket, a rakish, straw hat topped his head.

"Yes sir," Grover said, "we've got two hundred riders, now, not just fifty."

I couldn't help being distracted by an advertising poster that featured pictures of Cole, Frank and, just as prominently, Miss Edna Singer in those flesh-colored tights of hers.

Her flight through space occurred near the conclusion of things, but before it came cowboys and Indians, shooting exhibitions, and a mock gunfight—all first class. Cole couldn't participate in the show, since his parole forbade him from being in any theatrics. Instead, he sat in a specially constructed private box where he could reach out and shake hands with the customers or sign autographs.

Frank's part in things was a little more spectacular. Just before Miss Singer took center stage, Frank drove a stagecoach through the ring, fighting off a band of wild Apaches with his revolvers.

"Apaches are nothing compared to Pinkertons," he laughed, after the show.

The next season, 1906, I was sold to the White Sox for cash. It was a blow to my pride, at first, but I was glad once I had a chance to think it over. The Sox had a devil of a team— Big Ed Walsh, Doc White, Fielder Jones. The "hitless wonders" they called us. We put on a classic drive down the stretch, won the pennant, and beat the Cubs, four games to two, in the World Series.

In 1908, I was traded to the Indians, curiously enough, for that was the same year Cole quit the wildwest show. But they released me in the fall and when I got back home, Cole and I were both at loose ends.

"You know, Winfield," he said to me one day—Cole never called me Skeeter. "You know, Winfield, when I was in prison I said that someday I'd try to make up for some of the bad things I'd done and I reckon it's time I lived up to that promise."

The next spring, he went on the lecture circuit, his topic being the folly of crime and how it had ruined him. He peppered his speech with graphic descriptions of the horrors of prison life and frightened the wickedness out of more than one young man, I should imagine.

I played in the Southern Association that season, figuring it wouldn't be long before I was back in the major leagues. But in 1910 I hurt my back. I could still hit well enough, but I had trouble fielding grounders. I played in the Texas League for the next two years, where the heat was so bad I figured the next stop must be Hades.

Halfway through the 1912 season, I was hitting .178, had yet to steal a base and was finally forced to admit my days as a ballplayer were over. I went home, to Lee's Summit, without a cent, a job, or even a trade.

Grover, my little brother, owned part of a wild west show, himself, by that time. I could have worked for him, but I didn't find the idea appealing   My big brother, Sam, was selling Oldsmobiles in St. Louis, by then, and he said my notoriety as a ballplayer, humble as it was, would make selling cars easy. But I didn't like that idea, either.

After a while I started feeling pretty shiftless, so, just to keep occupied, I began keeping bees and bottling their honey. Cole had finished doing his lecture tours by this time, and pretty soon he became as fascinated with my bees as I was.

"Maybe you're not cut out to be a salesman," he said to me, one day, as we worked the hives. "Maybe this is what you're cut out for."

The bees were buzzing all around us.

"Beekeeping?" I complained. "Not much of a profession. People make a joke of it. Sam's making big money in St. Louis."

"Well, go to St. Louis, then," Cole said.

But two years later, I was still dawdling around with my bees, and it was around that time that we learned Frank James was ill. Cole knew what that meant, and I asked him if he wanted to go up to Kearney to visit to his old comrade, one last time.

"I don't suppose I could bear it," he said. "It all went by so fast."

When Frank died Cole took it pretty hard. A wire came. He opened it and read it. He went upstairs, lit his pipe, and just starred at the wall.

For the last year of his life Cole spent a lot of time cogitating on things. That summer his sister talked him into going to a revival meeting, and the Lord spoke in his heart. That night, Cole accepted Jesus and was baptized and saved.

He walked with a cane, by then, and couldn't get far. But if the weather was pleasant, he'd go sit on the porch and read his Bible. The cats would come around and, all afternoon, Cole and the cats would nap in the sunshine and study the birds winging their way from tree to tree.

Once, a woman came to see him. She was about sixty years of age, heavy set, and painted and powdered. She was somewhat unsteady on her feet, and two other women—her daughters they turned out to be—walked on each side of her, to help her keep her balance. They walked right up onto the front porch where Cole was sitting—I could see them from the yard—and introduced themselves.

The heavy woman seemed to start crying, but Cole, his eyes fixed on the floor, just kept shaking his head—no, no, no.

I asked him about it, later, but Cole was close mouthed. It wasn't until some months after that he revealed the heavy set woman was Darla Starr—daughter of Belle Starr, the famous outlaw.

"I knew Belle in Texas," he said, "and her daughter seems to have gotten it into her head that I'm her father. But Belle and I were never married, and I have no children. The woman's hounding me for money, that's all it is."

A few days before Cole died, I sat on the porch with him and the cats one last time. Cole had taken all the photographs he'd collected over the course of his life and put them into an album. Most of them were on thick pasteboard—studio portraits, taken before the days of the Kodak. He hadn't arranged them in the album oldest to newest, or in any sort of order, he'd just jumbled them all together in a way that made sense to him but no one else.

As we paged through the album, Cole talked about his life as an outlaw—about the bad things he'd done and how sorry he was. When we came across a photograph of Jesse—his expression grim—I figured it might be the last chance I'd ever have to learn the truth about something that had always plagued me.

"You know that story that used to go around about you and Jesse and Jim, when Jim was wounded after the Northfield Raid?"

"Yes," Cole nodded his head, "I suppose I've heard it."

"Is it true?" I said. "Did Jesse really want to kill Jim and bury him where the posses wouldn't find him?"

Cole thought for a moment. "Would it make any difference to you if he did?"

"Well, I don't guess Robin Hood ever tried to do anything like that."

"Good God, Winfield. Didn't you learn anything from my lectures? We weren't Robin Hoods. Frank once wondered if we'd even ceased to be human."

After Cole passed, I went to the city and tried selling Oldsmobiles. I was good at it, too. I'd tell the customers stories about Nap Lajoie and Addie Joss and, for some reason, they'd buy a car.

Then I met a girl—a farm girl, born and bred, but trapped in the city like I was. With our family's help, we managed to scrape together the wherewithal to buy a little place near Lee's Summit. Sam thought I was crazy.

"Farming isn't a paying proposition anymore."

"I suppose not," I said.

"And beekeeping, of all things."

We have children, now—six boys. We grow much of what we need and bottle our honey and sell that. On warm evenings we sit in the yard—just like Cole used to do—and I tell romantic tales about the James Gang and their adventures.

Frank and Jesse were driven to crime by injustice, I tell my boys. They only stole money from Yankees and never, ever, harmed a working man or a Southern woman. I tell them Jesse was loyal and gallant and honorable—that he robbed the rich to feed the poor—and that he isn't really dead, but only sleeping—like Arthur in Avalon—awaiting the time when we have need of him again.

Cole never would have approved.

EPILOGUE
Summer 1935
The Jesse James Scrapbook

Tom Gardner, age forty-one, climbed out of his government-issue Ford and eyeballed the dying farm. Dust in dunes covered the land, lay in drifts against the listing barn, the tumble-down house, and the windmill, becalmed and skeletal. He thought he'd seen despair in the soup kitchens and bread lines of Chicago and New York—in the faces of the little men huddled in alleys or selling pencils on street corners. But here, along the Oklahoma panhandle, it was hell on earth.

A rotting couch lay sprawled on the porch of the sway-backed farmhouse. A scrawny dog hid from the heat in its shadow. A woman, young but worn looking, watched from the door, a thumb sucking five year old braced against her hip.

"You from the gov'ment?"

"The W. P. A.," Tom told her.

"My husband's out gettin' work."

"Actually, I've come to see Mr. Hunter, Mr. J. J. Hunter. If he's up to it, that is."

"Oh, he's up to it, all right." The woman turned her head. "Grandpa..." she called. "We don't want no charity," she told Tom.

"I'm not from that part of the government," he explained. "I don't have anything to do with the Relief. I'm Works

Progress Administration, Federal Writer's Project. We're interviewing old timers before they... well, you know. Preserving our heritage, as it were."

"You know who he really is?"

"I know who he claims to be."

"You gonna make fun of him?"

Tom shook his head. "Wouldn't dream of it."

He'd never finished his old Jesse James Scrapbook, as he'd promised his mother he would, on that glorious summer day so long ago. But his mother, being a mother, hadn't had the heart to burn it, either. Instead, she'd hidden it away in an old steamer trunk, in the attic, and only given it back to him years later.

"He really is who he says he is," the worn woman told him.

"Maybe so," Tom said. Jesse would have been eighty-eight years old if he'd have lived, which, of course, he hadn't.

A sweaty, old man with yellow teeth, came out of the door and stepped onto the porch. He was frail but not bent, wrinkled but still spry.

Tom smiled. "Mr. Hunter?" He offered his hand, but the old man didn't take it.

"What's he want?"

"He's from the gov'ment," the woman said.

"Fed'l gov'ment?"

"W. P. A.," Tom volunteered.

The old man raised a single, shaking finger and stuck it, like a pistol, in Tom's face. "You tell Roosevelt I voted for him 'cause he said he'd give us back the money the bankers stole. You tell Roosevelt that when the dust blows up, our farms sink beneath it. Don't he know that?"

"Actually," Tom said. "I don't get to talk to him that often. I'm W. P. A., Federal Writer's Project. I just interview people."

"You a damn newspaper man?"

"Used to be," Tom said. "Before the Crash."

"Never had no use for newspaper men," the old man told the woman. "All they care about is money. All they do is lie."

"I know, Grandpa," the woman said.

"Look," Tom said. I'm not going to tell any lies, I just want to find out if you're who claim you are."

"That's just what I mean. I don't claim nothing. I was born in Clay County, Missouri, in 1847, and I'm the greatest outlaw ever lived."

"Robbed the rich to feed the poor, did you?"

"Goddamn right."

"Faked your own death to collect the reward money?"

"I got cheated out of that money. Bobby Ford, he cheated me. Charlie, too. All my life I been cheated. Even Roosevelt cheats me." He pointed at the government briefcase Tom carried. "You got money in there? Did Roosevelt send us our money? It's about goddamn time."

Tom shook his head. "I'm W. P. A. Understand? I'm not from Roosevelt. I don't have any money. All I got in here is shoes. Just shoes. No money. Just shoes."

The old man grinned and showed his broken teeth. "Shoes? What the hell you carryin' around shoes for? What you got shoes in a briefcase for?"

"Actually," Tom cracked, "they're glass slippers."

⌘

Inside the rotting farmhouse, a ten year old girl, skinny and cross, fried government potatoes on an old wood stove. A baby, diapered in flour sacks, scurried along the rough, wood floor. There was no electricity or running water. Red-brown, dust-bowl grit was everywhere, seeping through the cracks and gathering, in piles, on the windowsills.

"My wife, my mother, and my brother was the only ones knew the truth," the old man told Tom. "Bob and Charlie got hold of a dead man which looked like me, and the police wanted so hard to believe, they just went ahead and did. Easy to fool a man of something, if he wants to believe."

"Not always," Tom said.

The old man yelled at the little girl. "Bring me some coffee, and put some sugar in it."

She glared back. "Ain't got no sugar."

"She lies," the old man whispered.

After he'd faked his death, he told Tom, he'd owned a horse ranch in Wyoming. His second wife had cheated him out of that but, when Tom pressed him for details, he was vague about how she'd actually done it. After losing the horse ranch, he'd gone to Nevada where he'd married his third wife, lived with the Paiutes, and been made a chief—or so he claimed.

"Fourth wife come about in Pismo," he said. "Hollywood people all over the place in Pismo. Begged me to get into the picture shows with 'em, but I always turned 'em down. Mr. Douglas Fairbanks, hisself, come up to me diggin' clams one day and says 'Jesse, how was it God picked you to be the greatest outlaw ever?' And I says to him, 'Hell if I know, Doug, but pick me He did.'"

"It doesn't add up," Tom said. He pointed at the little girl. "The years. Your grandchildren. Do you have any proof?"

"I got my word, and my word is proof. Jesse James is me, and Jesse James don't lie." He picked up the coffee cup the girl had given Tom and sampled it without permission.

"She put sugar in your'n."

"Did not," the girl snapped back. "Ain't got no sugar," she told Tom.

"Do, too," the old man said.

Tom was tired of it all—the old man, the Depression, the poverty. He picked up his briefcase and set it on the table.

"I've got something to show you," he said.

The old man brightened and beamed like a child. "The glass slippers?"

"The shoes," Tom said.

"Shoes? Why the hell would Roosevelt send me shoes? I got more shoes than I can wear."

"They're special shoes," Tom said. "They're Jesse James' shoes."

"You got my shoes?"

"I got Jesse James' shoes."

He took them out of the briefcase and set them on the table. Once, they'd been quite something—patent leather, stylish, hand-tooled, very expensive—but now they were just old and worn.

"They're very small," Tom said. "Size six and a half. Think you can fit in Jesse James shoes?"

"'Course I can, but those ain't Jesse James' shoes, is all I'm tellin' you. They's too fancy. I never had no shoes like that. What the hell would Jesse James want with fancy shoes?"

"Jesse went dancing sometimes, didn't he?"

The old man threw back his head and opened his mouth. He squinted his eyes, as if towards the past. "Yes," he finally said. "I'd go dancing. But I never had no special shoes."

"I have it on good authority that these are, or were, Jesse James' shoes."

"You get 'em from her? You get 'em from Mary?"

"No," Tom said, but the name stopped him—Mary, Mary Rhawn. Tom had interviewed her once, in Russellville, Kentucky—a sweet old lady, who'd made a quilt about Jesse from old party dresses and embroidered it with shooting stars.

"She betrayed me," the old man said. "Whored around with Pony and Tot. Whores is all they were, all of them. All my life I been betrayed. Lied to. My father abandoned me when I was but three years old."

"Just try the shoes," Tom said, tired of it all.

The old man folded his arms across his chest. "They ain't my shoes, and I got corns."

"If they are your shoes, you've nothing to be afraid of."

"Who says they're my shoes?"

"I got them from a collector who got them from Frank."

The old man laughed. "Hell, Frank used to sell pebbles off my grave for fifty cents each. He'd scoop 'em out of the creek in the mornin' and sell 'em to tourists in the afternoon. You don't think a whore like Frank would be above doing the same with shoes, do you? What did you pay for them?"

"A hundred," Tom said.

"A hundred?" The old man broke into howls of laughter. "Hell, I'll sell you this whole damn farm for fifty. Those ain't my shoes. You been had, young man."

Later, Tom Gardner's government Ford bounced along the rutted lane that led away from the dying farm. By the time he turned onto the main highway, straight and endless, the black of night had fallen and a fat, full moon was in the sky.

At last, the old man had relented. He'd put his right leg on his left knee, picked up one of the shoes, and slipped it on as easy as butter.

"Told you I was Jesse James."

"I thought you said they weren't your shoes."

"That was before I knowed they'd fit."

Big, cross-country trucks rolled towards Tom, pinpoints of light, that grew sharper and more blinding, until they became roaring blurs that buffeted the little Ford. Above him, the vault of heaven was filled with an infinity of stars that shimmered like unborn souls, and, for a moment, Tom marveled at the immensity of it all—the stars, the void, the man in moon, wide-eyed and yawning.

The old man was as crazy as a loon, of course. Tom had seen hundreds like him since the Crash—addled old men who truly imagined themselves to be Jesse James, Billy the Kid, or George Armstrong Custer. They trembled like mice in doorways and on street corners, selling pencils for nickels. Tom would pay them, smile, and ponder for hours, how God could be so cruel.

Now, at the worst possible moment, when his mind was a million miles away, a red coyote, beautiful and running, emerged from the tar-black waste beyond the shoulder of the highway. It flared across the road, and appeared for an instant in the bright wedge the Ford's headlights made. Tom's heart leapt. He flicked the wheel and swerved the little car to avoid the animal, but it was already gone—a shooting star, that burst into light, then returned again, to the unknowable dark that marked the edge of all things.

Note on Sources

Although *The Jesse James Scrapbook* is a work of fiction, almost all of the incidents it depicts are based on actual, or at least legendary, incidents. For facts concerning the outlaws I have mainly relied on three well-documented books: *Jesse James Was His Name*, by William A. Settle, Jr., *The Outlaw Youngers, A Confederate Brotherhood*, and *Jesse James, the Man and the Myth*, both by Marley Brant.

Several other books, some very old, employ a more anecdotal approach to the James legend and provided much of the inspiration for the approach used here and for many of the incidents depicted. These include the works of Carl W. Breihan, the works of Homer Croy, *Jesse James, My Father*, by Jesse Edwards James, *The Rise and Fall of Jesse James*, by Robertus Love, and *The Life, Times, and Treacherous Death of Jesse James*, by Frank Triplett.

Many old issues of *The New York Times* contain contemporary accounts of the Civil War, the depredations of the guerrillas, and the careers of the outlaws. These were also inspirational and, in some instances, I have tried to preserve the tone of these articles in the fictitious ones I have written.

A number of other sources were useful in researching portions of the outlaw's careers. *My Life on the Frontier*, by Miguel Antonio Otero, and *Frontier Doctor*, by Henry F. Hoyt, both contain accounts of Jesse in Las Vegas, New Mexico. *Nat Goodwin's Book*, by entertainer Nat C. Goodwin, contains an account of a curious meeting with Bob Ford. *The Trial of Frank James for Murder*, published by Jingle Bob/Crown Publishers, contains a partial transcript of the trial at Gallatin and the confessions of two of the outlaws. *Convict Life at the Minnesota State Prison*, by William C. Heilbron, published by Valley History Press, includes a depiction of life in Stillwater Prison, and an account of the Northfield, Minnesota robbery written by Cole Younger. Letters written by Jesse and others—which form the inspiration for several of the fictitious letters here—can be found in a number of sources including *The New York Times*.

Many more sources were used to research the period in general. Among them were: *Black Slave Narratives*, edited by John F. Bayliss, *Quilter's Wisdom*, text by Eliza Calvert Hall, *Civil War on the Western Border*, by Jay Monaghan, *Everyday Life in the Wild West*, by Candy Moulton, *All God's Dangers*, compiled and edited by Theodore Rosengarten, *Riata and Spurs*, by western detective Charles Siringo, *The Brother's War: Civil War Letters*, edited by Anne Tapert, *Enter the Irish-American*, by Edward Wakin, and *Missouri, The WPA Guide to the "Show Me" State*, published by the Missouri Historical Society.

George Jansen has been a writer all his life. He has published short stories and poems, and collaborated on a half dozen technical books concerning computer languages, operating systems, and email.

When he was a boy, he worshipped the brave cowboys who roamed the wide-open movie screens of Oakland, California, where he was born. When he was five, he won honorary mention in a costume contest for his Hopalong Cassidy outfit. When he was twelve, he fell in love with the ghost towns of western Nevada and has been exploring them ever since. His first girlfriend taught him to ride, and his father, a Civil War buff, helped him appreciate the history of that terrible conflict and the haunted stillness that overhangs its battlefields.

Besides the West and Jesse James, George's interests include Bronze Age Europe, Mark Twain, and Arthurian Britain. He currently resides in Pleasant Hill, California with two big dogs and two fat cats.

Printed in the United States
31497LVS00013B/63